McCormick®

Cooking with
FLAVOR

Cooking with

FLAVOR

Contents

Publisher Richard Fraiman
General Manager Steven Sandonato
Executive Director, Marketing Services Carol Pittard
Director, Retail & Special Sales Tom Mifsud
Director, New Product Development Peter Harper
Assistant Director, Brand Marketing Laura Adam
Assistant General Counsel Dasha Smith Dwin
Marketing Manager Victoria Alfonso
Book Production Manager Suzanne Janso
Design & Prepress Manager Anne-Michelle Gallero

Special Thanks to Bozena Bannett, Alexandra Bliss, Glenn Buonocore, Robert Marasco, Brooke McGuire, Jonathan Polsky, Mary Sarro-Waite, Ilene Schreider, Adriana Tierno, Alex Voznesenskiy

Published by Time Inc. Home Entertainment

Time Inc.
1271 Avenue of the Americas
New York, New York 10020

ISBN 13: 978-1-933821-38-2
ISBN 10: 1-933821-38-8
Library of Congress #: 2007923881
Printed in China
We welcome your comments and suggestions.
Please write to us at:
McCormick Cooking with Flavor
Attention: Book Editors
PO Box 11016
Des Moines, IA 50336-1016

If you would like to order any of our hardcover Collector's Edition books, please call us at 1-800-327-6388. (Monday through Friday, 7:00 a.m.– 8:00 p.m. or Saturday, 7:00 a.m.– 6:00 p.m. Central Time).

McCormick Inc. US Consumer Product Division
Product Manager Céline Endler
Business Director Margaret Kime
Manager, McCormick Test Kitchens Theresa Kreinen
Senior Culinary Specialist Mary Beth Harrington

Copyright 2007
McCormick & Company, Inc.

Special Thanks McCormick Test Kitchens, McCormick Marketing Departments, McCormick Graphic Design Department, McCormick Market Research Department and McCormick Legal Department

Food Photography Michael Pohuski, with the exception of page 62, photo by Mark Thomas
Food Stylists Robin Lutz and Katrina Tekavec
Prop Stylist Colleen McIntosh

Spices, Herbs & Extracts Photography Mark Thomas

President Julie Merberg
Editor Sara Newberry
Design Elizabeth van Itallie

Special thanks Patty Brown, Pam Abrams, Dinah Dunn, Sarah Parvis, Kate Gibson

Spices cast a spell

on our imagination and flatter our senses with vibrant colors, enticing fragrances and distinctive flavors. The art and science of using spices and herbs began thousands of years ago when spices were considered more valuable than gold. Lands were discovered and the earth circled, all in the quest for spices.

These days, the spice buyers from McCormick® travel the globe to find the distinct and intriguing ingredients that every cook wants when they create in the kitchen. Those same aromatic spices and seasonings have been captured in every bottle, bringing your quest as close as your local grocery store.

For over 100 years, McCormick has been captivated and inspired by flavor and we wanted to share that passion with you. We know that the simplest way to transform a meal from ordinary to extraordinary is to cook with flavor. And it is in that spirit that we have created **McCormick Cooking with Flavor.**

We've combined our best easy-to-follow recipes, added interesting tidbits about spices and seasonings in the Enspicelopedia and mixed in our love of cooking to guarantee that this cookbook will **Spice Up Your Everyday Favorites.** And to make sure you have an assortment of delicious meal options, many of our recipes include Flavor Variations. Each additional flavor brings a new twist to the original dish, giving you more ways to create and savor new flavors! But the options don't end with the last page of our cookbook; you can visit www.mccormick.com to find even more ways to bring delectable flavors to your table.

Happy cooking!
The McCormick Test Kitchens

Breakfast & Brunch

Spicy pepper, **soothing** vanilla, **zesty** citrus . . . you'll love waking up to these flavors any day of the week!

Overnight French Toast

PREP TIME: 15 minutes · **REFRIGERATE:** 4 hours · **COOK TIME:** 25 minutes

5 eggs, beaten
¾ cup milk
1 tablespoon **Pure Vanilla Extract**
¼ teaspoon baking powder
1 loaf Italian bread, cut into 8 (1-inch-thick) slices
1 package (16 ounces) frozen whole strawberries, thawed
4 ripe bananas, sliced
1 cup granulated sugar
1 teaspoon **Cinnamon Sugar**

MIX eggs, milk, Pure Vanilla Extract and baking powder. Pour over bread to soak; turn to coat well. Cover. Refrigerate 4 hours or overnight.

MIX strawberries, bananas and granulated sugar in 13x9-inch baking dish. Top with soaked bread slices. Sprinkle with Cinnamon Sugar.

BAKE in preheated 450°F oven 20 to 25 minutes or until golden brown. Let stand 5 minutes before serving.

▶ **MAKES 8 SERVINGS**

flavor variations

■ **OVERNIGHT APPLE FRENCH TOAST**
Prepare and refrigerate bread slices as directed. Substitute 4 medium apples, cored, peeled and thinly sliced (about 4 cups) for the strawberries and bananas. Toss apples with 1 cup sugar and 1 teaspoon **Ground Cinnamon** in baking dish. Top with soaked bread slices. Sprinkle with Cinnamon Sugar. Cover with foil. Bake in preheated 375°F oven 30 minutes. Remove foil and bake 10 to 15 minutes longer or until apples are tender.

■ **QUICK & EASY FRENCH TOAST**
Mix 1 tablespoon sugar and 1 teaspoon **Ground Cinnamon** in medium bowl. Add 2 eggs and 2 teaspoons **Pure Vanilla Extract;** beat lightly to blend. Stir in ¼ cup milk. Dip 4 slices bread into egg mixture to coat both sides. Cook in melted butter in large skillet on medium heat until golden brown, turning once.

Cinnamon Pancakes

PREP TIME: 5 minutes · **COOK TIME:** 12 minutes

2 cups pancake mix
1 teaspoon **Ground Cinnamon**
2 eggs, beaten
1 cup milk
2 tablespoons vegetable oil
1 teaspoon **Pure Vanilla Extract**

STIR pancake mix and Ground Cinnamon in large bowl until well blended. Stir in eggs, milk, oil and Pure Vanilla Extract just until blended.

POUR ¼ cup batter per pancake onto preheated lightly greased griddle or skillet. Cook 1 to 2 minutes per side or until golden brown, turning when pancakes begin to bubble. Serve pancakes with Spiced Syrup (see recipe below), if desired.

► **MAKES 4 SERVINGS**

flavor variations

■ BLUEBERRY PANCAKES
Prepare batter as directed. Stir in 1 cup blueberries.

■ CINNAMON CHOCOLATE CHIP PANCAKES
Prepare batter as directed. Stir in ½ cup miniature chocolate chips after adding vanilla and eggs.

■ PECAN & PUMPKIN PIE SPICE PANCAKES
Prepare batter as directed. Use **Pumpkin Pie Spice** in place of the Ground Cinnamon and add 1 cup chopped pecans.

flavor addition

■ SPICED SYRUP
Mix 1 cup pancake syrup, 1 teaspoon **Pure Vanilla Extract** and ¼ teaspoon **Ground Cinnamon** or **Pumpkin Pie Spice** in microwavable measuring cup or bowl. Microwave on HIGH 1 to 2 minutes or until warm, stirring once.

Cinnamon Breadsticks

PREP TIME: 10 minutes · COOK TIME: 13 minutes

1 can (11 ounces) refrigerated breadsticks
2 tablespoons butter, melted
⅓ cup **Cinnamon Sugar***

*Or use ⅓ cup granulated sugar mixed with
1 teaspoon **Ground Cinnamon**

PREPARE breadsticks as directed on package. Pull each to about 6 inches in length.

BRUSH breadsticks with melted butter. Sprinkle each completely with Cinnamon Sugar. Twist and place on lightly greased baking sheet.

BAKE in preheated 375°F oven 10 to 13 minutes or until golden brown. Cool on wire rack.

► MAKES 6 SERVINGS

flavor addition

■ HOMEMADE FLAVORED COFFEE
Place ¾ cup ground coffee and ¼ cup firmly packed brown sugar in filter in brew basket of coffeemaker. Place 2 teaspoons **Pure Vanilla Extract** or **Raspberry Extract** in empty pot of coffeemaker. Add 6 cups water to coffeemaker; brew as directed.

Blueberry Muffins

PREP TIME: 15 minutes · COOK TIME: 25 minutes

2 cups flour
⅔ cup plus 2 tablespoons sugar
1½ teaspoons baking powder
½ teaspoon baking soda
¼ teaspoon salt
1 cup sour cream
¼ cup milk
¼ cup vegetable oil
1 egg, lightly beaten
1 teaspoon grated orange peel
1 teaspoon **Pure Vanilla Extract**
1 cup blueberries
½ teaspoon **Ground Cinnamon**

MIX flour, ⅔ cup sugar, baking powder, baking soda and salt in large bowl. Mix sour cream, milk, oil, egg, orange peel and Pure Vanilla Extract in medium bowl. Add to flour mixture; stir just until dry ingredients are moistened (batter will be thick and slightly lumpy). Gently stir in blueberries.

SPOON batter into 12 lightly greased or paper-lined muffin cups, filling each cup ⅔ full. Mix 2 tablespoons sugar and Ground Cinnamon. Sprinkle over muffins.

BAKE in preheated 400°F oven 20 to 25 minutes or until toothpick inserted into muffins comes out clean. Serve warm with Honey Butter (see recipe below), if desired.

► **MAKES 12 MUFFINS**

Ground Cinnamon

flavor variations

■ **APPLE MUFFINS**
Prepare batter as directed. Use 1 cup peeled, cored and chopped apple in place of the blueberries.

■ **RASPBERRY MUFFINS**
Prepare batter as directed. Use 1 cup raspberries in place of the blueberries.

flavor addition

■ **HONEY BUTTER**
Mix ½ cup (1 stick) butter, softened, 3 tablespoons honey, ½ teaspoon **Ground Cinnamon** and ¼ teaspoon **Ground Nutmeg** in small bowl until well blended and smooth.

Cinnamon Crumb Cake

PREP TIME: 20 minutes · COOK TIME: 35 minutes

2 cups flour
½ cup firmly packed brown sugar
½ cup granulated sugar
2 tablespoons **Ground Cinnamon**
1 cup (2 sticks) cold butter, cut
  into chunks
1 package (18¼ ounces) white
  cake mix
1 egg
1 cup sour cream
¼ cup (½ stick) butter, melted
1 teaspoon **Pure Vanilla Extract**

MIX flour, sugars and Ground Cinnamon in large bowl. Cut in 1 cup cold butter with pastry blender or 2 knives until mixture resembles coarse crumbs. Set aside.

BEAT cake mix, egg, sour cream, ¼ cup melted butter and Pure Vanilla Extract in large bowl with electric mixer on medium speed about 1 minute or just until mixed.

SPREAD evenly in greased and floured 13x9-inch baking pan. Sprinkle evenly with crumb mixture.

BAKE in preheated 350°F oven 30 to 35 minutes or until cake pulls away from sides of pan. Cool on wire rack. Cut into squares to serve.

► **MAKES 24 SERVINGS**

flavor variation

■ BLUEBERRY CRUMB CAKE
Prepare topping and batter as directed. Spread batter in baking pan. Sprinkle with 1 cup blueberries, then the crumb mixture. Bake 45 minutes.

flavor addition

■ CINNAMON COFFEE
Cinnamon Coffee is the perfect partner for this cake. Place ¾ cup ground coffee, ¼ cup firmly packed brown sugar and 2 teaspoons Ground Cinnamon in filter in brew basket of coffeemaker. Place ½ teaspoon Pure Vanilla Extract in empty pot of coffeemaker. Add 6 cups water to coffeemaker; brew as directed.

Cranberry Orange Bread

PREP TIME: 25 minutes · COOK TIME: 35 minutes

2 cups flour
1½ teaspoons baking powder
1 teaspoon **Ground Ginger**
½ teaspoon baking soda
½ teaspoon salt
¼ teaspoon **Ground Nutmeg**
⅓ cup (5⅓ tablespoons) butter, softened
1 cup sugar
1 teaspoon **Pure Vanilla Extract**
2 teaspoons grated orange peel
½ cup orange juice
2 eggs
1 cup coarsely chopped fresh cranberries
½ cup toasted slivered almonds

MIX flour, baking powder, Ground Ginger, baking soda, salt and Ground Nutmeg in large bowl.

BEAT butter, sugar and Pure Vanilla Extract in large bowl with electric mixer on medium speed until light and fluffy. Add orange peel, orange juice and eggs; mix well. Gradually add orange mixture to dry ingredients, mixing just until moistened. Gently stir in cranberries and almonds. Divide batter evenly among 3 greased 5½x3-inch loaf pans.

BAKE in preheated 350°F oven 35 minutes or until toothpick inserted in center comes out clean. Cool in pans 10 minutes. Remove from pans; cool completely on wire rack.

► **MAKES 3 LOAVES**

Ginger

flavor variations

■ TO USE DRIED CRANBERRIES
Cover 1 cup dried cranberries with 2 cups boiling water. Let stand 15 minutes. Drain before adding to batter.

■ TO PREPARE IN A 9X5-INCH LOAF PAN
Pour batter into 1 greased 9x5-inch loaf pan. Bake 55 to 60 minutes or until toothpick inserted in center comes out clean.

Chocolate Cinnamon Scones

PREP TIME: 15 minutes · COOK TIME: 30 minutes

2½ cups flour
⅔ cup sugar
2½ teaspoons baking powder
2 teaspoons **Ground Cinnamon**
½ teaspoon baking soda
¼ teaspoon salt
½ cup (1 stick) cold butter, cut into chunks
2 eggs
¾ cup sour cream
2 teaspoons **Pure Vanilla Extract**
6 ounces semisweet baking chocolate, chopped

MIX flour, sugar, baking powder, Ground Cinnamon, baking soda and salt in large bowl. Cut in cold butter with pastry blender or 2 knives until mixture resembles coarse crumbs.

BEAT eggs, sour cream and Pure Vanilla Extract in medium bowl with wire whisk until well blended. Add to flour mixture; stir until a soft dough forms. Stir in chopped chocolate.

PLACE dough on lightly floured surface. Knead about 1 minute or until smooth. Place dough on greased baking sheet. Pat into a 10-inch round. Score top of dough with sharp knife into 12 wedges.

BAKE in preheated 375°F oven 30 minutes or until golden brown. Cool slightly on wire rack. Melt and drizzle additional semisweet chocolate over scones, if desired. Cut into 12 wedges to serve.

► **MAKES 12 SCONES**

flavor variations

■ **DROP SCONES**
Prepare dough as directed. Drop ¼ cupfuls 2 inches apart on greased baking sheet. Bake 20 minutes or until golden brown.

■ **CRANBERRY WALNUT SCONES**
Prepare as directed. Use **Pumpkin Pie Spice** in place of the Ground Cinnamon. Substitute ½ cup <u>each</u> dried cranberries <u>and</u> chopped walnuts for the chopped chocolate. Sprinkle with 2 teaspoons sugar.

■ **PECAN RAISIN SCONES**
Prepare as directed. Use **Pumpkin Pie Spice** in place of the Ground Cinnamon. Substitute ½ cup <u>each</u> chopped pecans <u>and</u> golden raisins for the chocolate. Sprinkle with 2 teaspoons sugar.

Very Vanilla Fruit Salad

PREP TIME: 15 minutes · REFRIGERATE: 1 hour

2 cups strawberries, halved
1 cup blueberries
1 cup fresh or canned pineapple chunks
1 cup cantaloupe chunks
2 kiwis, peeled and sliced
¼ cup confectioners' sugar
2 teaspoons **Pure Vanilla Extract**

MIX fruit, confectioners' sugar and Pure Vanilla Extract in large bowl.

REFRIGERATE 1 hour or until ready to serve.

► **MAKES 10 SERVINGS**

flavor variation

■ RASPBERRY FRUIT SALAD
Prepare fruit salad as directed. Use
Raspberry Extract in place of the
Pure Vanilla Extract.

Italian Herb Frittata

PREP TIME: 15 minutes · COOK TIME: 15 minutes

1 tablespoon olive oil
1 medium onion, chopped
1 medium zucchini, halved lengthwise and
  cut into ¼-inch-thick slices
1 cup diced ham
6 eggs
¼ cup milk
1 teaspoon **Italian Seasoning**
¼ teaspoon salt
¼ teaspoon **Ground Black Pepper**
2 medium plum tomatoes, sliced
1 cup shredded mozzarella cheese

HEAT oil in large ovenproof nonstick skillet on medium heat. Add onion and zucchini; cook and stir 2 minutes. Reduce heat to medium-low. Add ham; cook 2 minutes.

BEAT eggs, milk, Italian Seasoning, salt and Ground Black Pepper in medium bowl. Pour mixture into skillet. Cook without stirring 5 minutes or until eggs are just set on bottom. Arrange sliced tomatoes on top of egg mixture. Sprinkle with cheese.

BROIL 4 to 5 minutes until eggs are set and cheese is lightly browned. Sprinkle with additional Italian Seasoning, if desired.

► **MAKES 6 SERVINGS**

flavor variations

■ SAUSAGE FRITTATA
Prepare frittata as directed. Use 1 cup coarsely chopped red and/or green bell pepper and 1 cup refrigerated shredded potatoes in place of the zucchini. Omit ham and add 1 cup crumbled cooked sausage to egg mixture. Substitute 1 teaspoon **Basil Leaves** for the Italian Seasoning and omit tomatoes.

■ SMOKED SALMON FRITTATA
Prepare frittata as directed. Use 12 asparagus spears, ends trimmed and cut into ½-inch pieces (about 1 cup) in place of the zucchini. Omit ham and add 1 cup coarsely chopped smoked salmon to egg mixture. Substitute 1 teaspoon **Dill Weed** for the Italian Seasoning. Use 1 cup shredded Swiss cheese in place of the mozzarella cheese and omit tomatoes.

Country Breakfast Casserole

PREP TIME: 15 minutes · COOK TIME: 40 minutes

1 roll (12 ounces) breakfast sausage,
  cooked, crumbled and drained
2 cups shredded Cheddar cheese
6 eggs, lightly beaten
1 cup water
½ cup milk
1 package **Original Country Gravy Mix** or
  Sausage Country Gravy Mix
6 slices bread, cut into 1-inch cubes
2 tablespoons melted butter (optional)
Paprika

SPREAD cooked sausage over bottom of lightly greased 11x7-inch baking dish. Sprinkle cheese over sausage.

STIR eggs, water, milk and Gravy Mix in medium bowl with whisk until well blended. Pour over cheese. Arrange bread cubes evenly over mixture. Drizzle butter over bread, if desired. Sprinkle with Paprika.

BAKE, uncovered, in preheated 325°F oven 40 minutes or until knife inserted in center comes out clean. Remove from oven. Let stand 10 minutes before serving.

► MAKES 8 SERVINGS

make-ahead tip

■ Prepare casserole as directed, but do not bake. Cover and refrigerate unbaked casserole overnight. Bake, uncovered, 50 minutes or until knife inserted in center comes out clean.

Paprika

Breakfast Burritos

PREP TIME: 10 minutes · COOK TIME: 5 minutes

4 eggs
¼ cup milk
1 cup cubed cooked ham
½ teaspoon **Season-All® Seasoned Salt**
½ teaspoon **Coarse Ground Black Pepper**
1 tablespoon butter
4 flour tortillas (burrito-size)
1 cup shredded Mexican-blend cheese

BEAT eggs and milk in large bowl. Add ham, Season-All Seasoned Salt and Coarse Ground Black Pepper; mix well.

MELT butter in large nonstick skillet on medium heat. Add egg mixture; cook and stir until eggs are firm.

SPOON egg mixture into each warmed flour tortilla. Top each with ¼ cup of the cheese. Fold into burritos to serve.

► MAKES 4 SERVINGS

flavor variations

■ GARLIC PEPPER BREAKFAST BURRITOS
Prepare egg mixture as directed. Use 1 teaspoon **California Style® Garlic Pepper** in place of the Season-All Seasoned Salt and Coarse Ground Black Pepper.

■ CHILI BREAKFAST BURRITOS
Prepare egg mixture as directed. Use ¼ teaspoon **Chili Powder** in place of the Season-All Seasoned Salt and Coarse Ground Black Pepper.

Coarse Black Pepper

Appetizers

Whether your taste runs **spicy** or **subtle, peppery** or **garlicky, tangy** or **zesty**—here is a selection of tantalizing starters.

Classic Hummus

PREP TIME: 10 minutes

1 can (15 ounces) chickpeas
1 tablespoon **California Style® Minced Wet Garlic**
1 tablespoon lemon juice
1 teaspoon **Ground Cumin**
¼ teaspoon **Crushed Red Pepper**
¼ teaspoon salt
Olive oil
Chopped green onions, chopped olives, <u>or</u> chopped tomato, for garnish (optional)

DRAIN chickpeas, reserving ¼ cup of the liquid. Place chickpeas, Minced Wet Garlic, lemon juice, Ground Cumin, Crushed Red Pepper and salt in food processor; cover. Process until smooth, scraping down sides as necessary. Add reserved chickpea liquid; process until smooth.

DRIZZLE hummus with olive oil. Garnish with chopped green onions, chopped olives or chopped tomato, if desired. Serve with pita chips or warm pita wedges. Store hummus in airtight container in refrigerator up to 2 days.

► **MAKES 1¼ CUPS**

flavor variations

■ HUMMUS WITH TAHINI
Prepare as directed. Add 2 tablespoons tahini (sesame seed paste) with the Minced Wet Garlic.

■ Prepare as directed. Use 2 teaspoons **Garlic Powder** in place of the Minced Wet Garlic. Reserve ⅓ cup of the chickpea liquid.

■ BRUSCHETTA WITH HUMMUS AND ROASTED RED PEPPER
(see recipe on page 38).

Ground Cumin

Creamy Dill Dip

PREP TIME: 5 minutes · REFRIGERATE: 1 hour

1 cup sour cream
1 teaspoon **Celery Salt**
1 teaspoon **Dill Weed**
⅛ teaspoon **Onion Powder**

MIX sour cream, Celery Salt, Dill Weed and Onion Powder in medium bowl until well blended. Cover.

REFRIGERATE at least 1 hour to blend flavors. Serve as a dip with assorted cut-up vegetables or crackers.

► **MAKES 1 CUP**

flavor variations

■ CREAMY ITALIAN DIP
Prepare as directed. Omit Celery Salt and Dill Weed. Stir ½ teaspoon **Garlic Salt** and ¼ teaspoon **Italian Seasoning** into the sour cream mixture.

■ ROASTED RED PEPPER DIP
Prepare as directed. Omit Celery Salt. Stir 1 cup mayonnaise, 1 jar (7 ounces) roasted red peppers, drained and finely chopped, and ½ teaspoon **Garlic Salt** into sour cream mixture.

■ SPINACH DIP
Prepare as directed. Omit Celery Salt. Stir 1 cup mayonnaise and 1 package (10 ounces) frozen chopped spinach, thawed, drained and squeezed dry, into sour cream mixture.

OLD BAY Hot Crab Dip

PREP TIME: 10 minutes · **COOK TIME:** 30 minutes

1 package (8 ounces) cream cheese,
   softened
1 cup mayonnaise
2 teaspoons **OLD BAY® Seasoning**
½ teaspoon **Ground Mustard**
1 pound jumbo lump crabmeat
¼ cup shredded Cheddar cheese

MIX cream cheese, mayonnaise, OLD BAY Seasoning and Ground Mustard in medium bowl until well blended and smooth. Add crabmeat; toss gently.

SPREAD in 9-inch pie plate. Sprinkle with cheese and additional OLD BAY Seasoning, if desired.

BAKE in preheated 350°F oven 30 minutes or until hot and bubbly. Serve with assorted crackers or sliced French bread.

► **MAKES 3½ CUPS**

Ground Mustard

flavor variations

■ **HOT ARTICHOKE DIP**
Prepare as directed. Omit OLD BAY Seasoning, crabmeat and Cheddar cheese. Stir 1 can (14 ounces) artichoke hearts, drained and chopped, ½ cup grated Parmesan cheese and 1 teaspoon **Garlic Powder** into cream cheese mixture. Bake as directed.

Seven Layer Dip

PREP TIME: 15 minutes

1 can (**16 ounces**) refried beans
1 container (**16 ounces**) sour cream
1 package **Taco Seasoning Mix**
2 cups (**8 ounces**) shredded Cheddar cheese
1 cup prepared guacamole
1 cup chopped tomatoes
½ cup sliced green onions
½ cup sliced black olives

SPREAD refried beans in shallow serving dish.

MIX sour cream and Taco Seasoning Mix in small bowl until well blended. Spread over refried beans.

TOP with cheese, dollops of guacamole, tomato, onions and olives. Serve with tortilla chips.

► **MAKES 8 CUPS**

Mediterranean Salsa

PREP TIME: 10 minutes

1 cup finely chopped plum tomatoes
2 tablespoons olive oil
1 tablespoon cider vinegar
2 teaspoons **Basil Leaves**
1 teaspoon **Oregano Leaves**
½ teaspoon **Onion Salt**

MIX tomatoes, oil, vinegar, Basil Leaves, Oregano Leaves and Onion Salt in medium bowl. Let stand at room temperature 30 minutes to blend flavors.

SERVE with pita chips.

► MAKES 1 CUP

flavor variations

■ GREEK SALSA
Stir ¼ cup crumbled feta cheese and ¼ teaspoon **Dried Mint Flakes** into the tomato mixture.

■ ITALIAN SALSA
Substitute 1½ teaspoons **Italian Seasoning** and ½ teaspoon **Garlic Powder** for the Basil Leaves, Oregano Leaves and Onion Salt.

■ MEDITERRANEAN BRUSCHETTA
(see recipe on page 38).

Oregano

Italian Bread Dipping Oil

PREP TIME: 5 minutes

8 twists **Sea Salt Grinder**
1 teaspoon grated Parmesan cheese
½ teaspoon **Garlic Powder**
⅛ teaspoon **Crushed Red Pepper**
¼ cup extra-virgin olive oil

TWIST Sea Salt Grinder over a small shallow dish. Add Parmesan cheese, Garlic Powder and Crushed Red Pepper.

POUR oil over spices. Gently swirl dish to moisten.

SERVE as a dipping sauce with crusty bread.

► **MAKES 4 SERVINGS**

Crushed Red Pepper

Garlic

flavor variation

■ HERB BREAD DIPPING OIL
Prepare as directed. Omit Crushed Red Pepper. Stir ¼ teaspoon **Italian Seasoning** or **Rosemary Leaves**, crushed, into oil mixture.

Spiced Shrimp Cocktail

PREP TIME: 5 minutes · COOK TIME: 3 minutes

½ cup cider vinegar <u>or</u> beer
½ cup water
2 tablespoons **OLD BAY® Seasoning**
1 pound large shrimp, peeled and deveined, leaving tails on
1 cup **Seafood Cocktail Sauce**

MIX vinegar, water and OLD BAY Seasoning in medium saucepan. Bring to boil on medium heat. Gently stir in shrimp; cover.

SIMMER 2 to 3 minutes or just until shrimp turn pink. Drain well.

SERVE immediately or refrigerate until ready to serve. Serve with Seafood Cocktail Sauce.

► **MAKES 8 SERVINGS**

Confetti Bites

PREP TIME: 15 minutes · **COOK TIME:** 15 minutes

2 packages (8 ounces <u>each</u>) refrigerated crescent rolls
2 packages (8 ounces <u>each</u>) cream cheese, softened
¼ cup mayonnaise
½ teaspoon **Basil Leaves**
¼ teaspoon **Garlic Powder**
1½ cups chopped vegetables, such as green and red bell peppers, carrots and broccoli
2 tablespoons **Salad Supreme®** **Seasoning**

UNROLL dough onto 15x10x1-inch baking sheet. Press perforations to seal. Bake in preheated 350°F oven 12 to 15 minutes or until golden brown. Cool completely on wire rack.

MIX cream cheese, mayonnaise, Basil Leaves and Garlic Powder until well blended and smooth. Spread evenly in a thin layer over cooled crust. Top with chopped vegetables. Sprinkle generously with Salad Supreme Seasoning.

SERVE immediately or refrigerate until ready to serve. Cut into 2-inch squares to serve.

► **MAKES 35 SERVINGS**

flavor variations

■ MEXICAN CONFETTI BITES
Substitute 1 package **Taco Seasoning Mix** for the Basil Leaves, Garlic Powder and Salad Supreme Seasoning. Sprinkle cream cheese mixture with 1½ cups finely chopped tomatoes, 1 cup shredded Cheddar <u>or</u> Mexican cheese blend and ½ cup <u>each</u> thinly sliced black olives <u>and</u> green onions.

■ DESSERT CONFETTI BITES
Prepare dough as directed. Omit mayonnaise, Basil Leaves, Garlic Powder and Salad Supreme Seasoning. Beat 1 cup confectioners' sugar and 1 teaspoon <u>each</u> **Pure Lemon Extract** <u>and</u> **Pure Vanilla Extract** into softened cream cheese until well blended and smooth. Gently stir in 1 cup thawed frozen whipped topping. Spread over crust. Arrange 3 cups assorted fresh berries over the cream cheese mixture.

Party Pizza

PREP TIME: 15 minutes · COOK TIME: 10 minutes

1 (12-inch) or 2 (8-inch) prepared pizza
  crusts
1 cup shredded Mozzarella cheese
¼ cup grated Parmesan cheese
1 cup thinly sliced vegetables, such as red
  bell pepper, zucchini and mushrooms
1 tablespoon olive oil
1 teaspoon **Italian Seasoning**
¼ teaspoon **Garlic Powder**
¼ cup sliced black olives

PLACE pizza crust on large baking sheet.

MIX mozzarella and Parmesan cheeses in small bowl. Toss vegetables, ½ of the cheese mixture, oil, Italian Seasoning and Garlic Powder in medium bowl. Spread mixture evenly over crust. Sprinkle with olives and remaining cheese mixture.

BAKE in preheated 450°F oven 8 to 10 minutes or until cheese is melted. Cut into 2-inch pieces to serve.

► **MAKES 16 SERVINGS**

flavor variations

■ TOMATO PARTY PIZZA
Substitute 1 cup coarsely chopped tomatoes for the sliced vegetables.

■ TEX-MEX PARTY PIZZA
Substitute 1½ cups shredded Mexican cheese blend for the mozzarella and Parmesan cheeses. Use 1 cup coarsely chopped tomatoes and ¼ cup chopped red onion for the sliced vegetables. Use 2 teaspoons **Chili Powder** and 1 teaspoon hot pepper sauce in place of the Italian Seasoning.

Caribbean Shrimp Bruschetta

PREP TIME: 15 minutes · **COOK TIME:** 10 minutes

1 pound cooked peeled shrimp, coarsely
   chopped
1 cup shredded Monterey Jack cheese
1 mango, peeled and chopped (about 1 cup)
¼ cup finely chopped red bell pepper
¼ cup sliced green onions
2 tablespoons lime juice
½ teaspoon **Ground Allspice**
½ teaspoon **Thyme Leaves**
¼ teaspoon **Crushed Red Pepper**
¼ teaspoon salt
32 Bruschetta Toasts (see recipe below)

MIX all ingredients, except Bruschetta Toasts, in large bowl until well blended.

SPOON shrimp mixture evenly onto Bruschetta Toasts.

BAKE in preheated 400°F oven 8 to 10 minutes or until heated through and cheese is melted.

► **MAKES 32 SERVINGS**

flavor variations

■ **BRUSCHETTA TOASTS**
Slice 1 loaf French bread into 32 (½-inch-thick) slices. Lightly brush both sides of each bread slice with olive oil. Place in single layer on baking sheet. Bake in preheated 425°F oven 6 to 8 minutes or until lightly browned and crisp, turning once. Cool on wire rack. If not using immediately, store cooled toasts in airtight container.

■ **BRUSCHETTA WITH HUMMUS AND ROASTED RED PEPPER**
Prepare Classic Hummus as directed (see recipe on page 26). Spread 24 Bruschetta Toasts with hummus. Top each with a shaving of Manchego cheese and a strip of roasted red pepper.

■ **MEDITERRANEAN BRUSCHETTA**
Prepare Mediterranean Salsa as directed (see recipe on page 31). Stir in ¼ cup chopped black olives. Spread each of 15 Bruschetta Toasts with 1 teaspoon soft goat cheese. Top each with 1 tablespoon Mediterranean Salsa.

Main Dishes

From **quick and easy** one-dish meals to elegant **herb-crusted** roasts, here's a selection of **flavorful favorites** to satisfy any palate.

Rosemary Roasted Chicken

PREP TIME: 5 minutes · **COOK TIME:** 1½ hours

1 whole chicken (about 3 pounds)
1 tablespoon olive oil
2 teaspoons **Rosemary Leaves,** crushed
2 teaspoons **Season-All® Seasoned Salt**
½ teaspoon **Thyme Leaves**

Perfect Chicken Gravy (see recipe below)

PLACE chicken on rack in foil-lined roasting pan. Brush with oil.

MIX Rosemary Leaves, Season-All Seasoned Salt and Thyme Leaves in small bowl. Rub evenly over entire chicken.

ROAST in preheated 375°F oven 1 to 1½ hours or until chicken is cooked through. Serve with Perfect Chicken Gravy, if desired.

► **MAKES 6 SERVINGS**

Rosemary

flavor addition

■ PERFECT CHICKEN GRAVY
Pour ½ cup drippings from roasting pan and 1½ cups water into medium saucepan. Stir in 2 packages **Chicken Gravy Mix.** Stirring frequently, cook on medium heat until gravy comes to boil. Reduce heat to low; simmer 1 minute or until slightly thickened. (Gravy will thicken upon standing.)

flavor variation

■ PEPPERED ROASTED CHICKEN
Prepare as directed. Omit Rosemary Leaves. Stir 1 teaspoon **Ground Black Pepper** and ⅛ teaspoon **Ground Red Pepper** into seasoning mixture.

Lemon Garlic Chicken

PREP TIME: 10 minutes · COOK TIME: 20 minutes

¼ cup flour
½ teaspoon salt
½ teaspoon **Ground Black Pepper**
1 pound thinly sliced boneless, skinless chicken breast halves
3 tablespoons olive oil, divided
2 tablespoons white wine
1 tablespoon **California Style® Wet Garlic**
1 cup chicken broth
¼ cup lemon juice

MIX flour, salt and Ground Black Pepper on plate. Moisten chicken lightly with water. Coat evenly with flour mixture.

HEAT 2 tablespoons of the oil in large nonstick skillet on medium-high heat. Cook chicken, several pieces at a time, 3 minutes per side or until golden brown. Add remaining 1 tablespoon oil as needed. Remove chicken from skillet; keep warm.

ADD wine and California Style Wet Garlic to skillet, scraping up brown bits from bottom of skillet. Stir in chicken broth and lemon juice. Bring to boil on medium heat. Reduce heat and simmer 5 minutes or until sauce is reduced by half. Spoon sauce over chicken to serve. Serve with Savory Orzo (see recipe on page 90), if desired.

► **MAKES 4 SERVINGS**

Garlic

flavor variation

■ LEMON PEPPER CHICKEN
Prepare as directed. Use 2 tablespoons **Lemon & Pepper Seasoning Salt** in place of the salt and Ground Black Pepper. Omit lemon juice.

Oven-Fried Chicken

PREP TIME: 5 minutes · COOK TIME: 20 minutes

¼ cup flour
1½ teaspoons **Season-All®
Seasoned Salt**
½ teaspoon **Oregano Leaves**
¼ teaspoon **Ground Black Pepper**
1¼ pounds boneless skinless
chicken breast halves <u>or</u> thighs
¼ cup milk
1 tablespoon butter, melted

SPRAY 15x10x1-inch baking pan with nonstick cooking spray.

MIX flour, Season-All Seasoned Salt, Oregano Leaves and Ground Black Pepper on large plate. Moisten chicken with milk. Coat evenly with flour mixture. Place chicken in single layer in prepared baking pan. Drizzle with melted butter.

BAKE in preheated 425°F oven 15 to 20 minutes or until chicken is cooked through.

▶ **MAKES 5 SERVINGS**

flavor variations

■ ITALIAN OVEN-FRIED CHICKEN
Use 1 teaspoon **Italian Seasoning** in place of the Oregano Leaves.

■ OVEN-FRIED CHICKEN WITH ROSEMARY
Use 1 teaspoon **Rosemary Leaves,** crushed in place of the Oregano Leaves.

Oregano

Onion Baked Chicken

PREP TIME: 10 minutes · COOK TIME: 50 minutes

1 tablespoon **Onion Powder**
1½ teaspoons **Garlic Salt**
1½ teaspoons **Italian Seasoning**
½ teaspoon **Paprika**
3 to 3½ pounds chicken parts
1 tablespoon oil

MIX Onion Powder, Garlic Salt, Italian Seasoning and Paprika in small bowl.

BRUSH chicken with oil. Coat chicken evenly with seasoning mixture. Place chicken in shallow baking pan.

BAKE in preheated 375°F oven 45 to 50 minutes or until chicken is cooked through.

► MAKES 8 SERVINGS

Spicy White Bean & Chicken Chili

PREP TIME: 10 minutes · COOK TIME: 20 minutes

2 tablespoons oil
1½ pounds boneless, skinless chicken
   breasts, cut into ½-inch cubes
½ cup chopped onion
2 teaspoons **Ground Cumin**
1½ teaspoons **Garlic Salt**
¾ teaspoon **Oregano Leaves**
¼ teaspoon **Chili Powder**
¼ teaspoon **Ground Red Pepper**
1 can (14½ ounces) white beans, undrained
1 can (4½ ounces) chopped green chiles,
   drained
½ cup chicken broth
Assorted toppings such as sour cream,
   sliced green onions, sliced jalapeño
   peppers and chopped tomatoes (optional)

HEAT oil in large skillet on medium-high heat. Add chicken and onion; cook and stir 5 minutes or until lightly browned.

STIR in Ground Cumin, Garlic Salt, Oregano Leaves, Chili Powder, Ground Red Pepper, beans, chiles and broth until well blended. Bring to boil. Reduce heat to low; simmer 10 to 15 minutes, stirring occasionally. Serve with assorted toppings, if desired.

► **MAKES 4 SERVINGS**

Classic Chicken Paprika

PREP TIME: 10 minutes · COOK TIME: 25 minutes

1 pound boneless, skinless chicken thighs
2½ teaspoons **Paprika,** divided
½ teaspoon salt
⅛ teaspoon **Ground Black Pepper**
1 tablespoon olive oil
1 medium onion, coarsely chopped
   (about 1 cup)
1 can (14½ ounces) diced tomatoes,
   undrained
⅓ cup light cream
Egg noodles, prepared according to
   package directions

SEASON chicken with ½ teaspoon of the Paprika, salt and Ground Black Pepper.

HEAT oil in large nonstick skillet on medium-high heat. Add chicken; cook 3 minutes per side or until browned. Remove chicken from skillet. Add onion to skillet; cook and stir 3 minutes.

STIR in tomatoes and remaining 2 teaspoons Paprika. Bring to boil. Return chicken to skillet. Reduce heat to low; cover and simmer 15 minutes or until chicken is cooked through. Stir in cream until well blended. Serve over egg noodles.

► **MAKES 4 SERVINGS**

Chicken Cacciatore

PREP TIME: 15 minutes · COOK TIME: 20 minutes

¼ cup flour
½ teaspoon salt
⅛ teaspoon **Ground Black Pepper**
1 pound boneless skinless chicken breasts,
cut into 1-inch cubes
3 tablespoons olive oil, divided
1 package (10 ounces) sliced mushrooms
1 medium green bell pepper, cut into strips
(about 1 cup)
1 medium onion, coarsely chopped
(about 1 cup)
2 tablespoons **California Style® Wet
Garlic**
1 can (14½ ounces) stewed tomatoes,
undrained and cut up
1 can (8 ounces) tomato sauce
1½ teaspoons **Italian Seasoning**

MIX flour, salt and Ground Black Pepper on plate. Coat chicken evenly with flour mixture.

HEAT 2 tablespoons of the oil in large skillet on medium-high heat. Add chicken; cook and stir 5 minutes or until lightly browned. Remove chicken from skillet. Add remaining 1 tablespoon oil to skillet. Add mushrooms, bell pepper, onion and California Style Wet Garlic; cook and stir 5 minutes on medium heat or until vegetables are tender.

STIR in tomatoes, tomato sauce and Italian Seasoning. Bring to boil, stirring frequently. Return chicken to skillet. Reduce heat to low; cover and simmer 5 minutes or until chicken is heated through. Serve over pasta or rice, if desired.

► **MAKES 6 SERVINGS**

Black Peppercorns

flavor variations
■ Substitute 1 teaspoon **Garlic Powder** for the California Style Wet Garlic.

Sour Cream Chicken Enchiladas

PREP TIME: 20 minutes · COOK TIME: 1 hour

2 packages **Enchilada Sauce Mix**
3½ cups milk
1 cup sour cream
1 can (4½ ounces) chopped green chiles, drained
2 tablespoons oil, divided
1 pound boneless, skinless chicken breasts, cut into thin strips
1 medium onion, thinly sliced
1 medium bell pepper, cut into thin strips
10 flour <u>or</u> corn tortillas
2 cups shredded Mexican-blend cheese

STIR Enchilada Sauce Mix and milk in medium saucepan. Stirringly constantly, cook on medium heat 5 minutes or until thickened. Stir in sour cream and chiles. Set aside.

HEAT 1 tablespoon of the oil in large skillet on medium heat. Add chicken; cook and stir 3 minutes or until lightly browned. Remove from skillet. In same skillet, heat remaining 1 tablespoon oil. Add onion and bell pepper; cook and stir 5 minutes or until tender. Return chicken to skillet. Stir in ½ cup of the sauce.

SPREAD ½ cup of sauce in lightly greased 13x9-inch baking dish. Heat tortillas as directed on package. Divide chicken mixture evenly among tortillas. Fold over tortilla sides; place seam-side down in baking dish. Pour remaining sauce over enchiladas. Sprinkle with cheese.

BAKE in preheated 325°F oven 40 minutes or until heated through and cheese is melted.

► **MAKES 10 SERVINGS**

flavor variation

■ BEEF ENCHILADAS
Mix 1 can (8 ounces) tomato sauce, 1½ cups water and 1 package **Enchilada Sauce Mix** in medium saucepan. Bring to boil. Reduce heat to low; simmer 5 minutes. Set aside. Brown 1 pound ground beef in medium skillet on medium-high heat. Drain fat. Stir ½ cup sauce into meat. Coat each of 8 corn tortillas with sauce. Spoon 3 tablespoons meat mixture down center of each tortilla. Fold over tortilla sides; place seam-side down in lightly greased 12x8-inch baking dish. Spoon remaining sauce over enchiladas. Sprinkle with 1 cup shredded Cheddar cheese. Bake in preheated 350°F oven 15 minutes or until heated through and cheese is melted. Makes 8 servings.

Sage-Rubbed Turkey Breast

PREP TIME: 10 minutes · COOK TIME: 2½ hours

1 tablespoon **Rubbed Sage**
1½ teaspoons **Season-All®**
  Seasoned Salt
½ teaspoon **Ground Black Pepper**
1 turkey breast, fresh or frozen, thawed
  (5 to 6 pounds)
1 cup water

MIX Rubbed Sage, Season-All Seasoned Salt and Ground Black Pepper in small bowl.

PLACE turkey breast on rack in foil-lined roasting pan. Spread seasoning mixture over entire surface and under skin of turkey breast. Cover loosely with heavy duty foil.

ROAST in preheated 350°F oven 1 hour. Remove foil and add water. Roast, basting occasionally with pan juices, 1 to 1½ hours longer or until internal temperature reaches 170°F. Remove from oven and cover loosely with foil. Let stand 15 minutes. Transfer to platter or carving board and slice. Serve with Perfect Turkey Gravy (see recipe on page 152) and Harvest Roasted Vegetables (see recipe on Page 85).

► **MAKES 10 SERVINGS**

flavor variation
■ ITALIAN ROASTED TURKEY BREAST
Substitute 1 tablespoon **Italian Seasoning** for the Rubbed Sage.

flavor addition
■ SPICED PEAR AND RAISIN CHUTNEY
Serve alongside turkey breast. Place 1 cup pomegranate juice, ¼ cup packed brown sugar, ½ teaspoon **Ground Cinnamon**, ¼ teaspoon each **Ground Allspice, Pure Vanilla Extract** and **Pure Orange Extract** in medium saucepan. Cook on medium heat until sugar is dissolved, stirring occasionally. Add 2 pears, peeled and cut into ½-inch chunks, and 1 cup each dried apricots, quartered, and raisins. Simmer 5 minutes or until raisins are plumped and mixture is slightly thickened. Store, covered, in refrigerator up to 1 week.

Turkey Pot Pie

PREP TIME: 5 minutes · COOK TIME: 40 minutes

2 packages **Turkey Gravy Mix**
1 teaspoon **Poultry Seasoning**
1½ cups milk
1 cup water
2 tablespoons butter
3 cups cubed cooked turkey <u>or</u> chicken
2 cups frozen mixed vegetables
1 refrigerated pie crust (from 15-ounce package)

MIX Turkey Gravy Mix, Poultry Seasoning, milk, water and butter in large skillet or saucepan. Bring to boil on medium heat, stirring frequently. Stir in turkey and vegetables. Return to boil. Reduce heat to low; simmer 5 minutes.

SPOON into 9-inch deep-dish pie plate or 2-quart baking dish. Top with pie crust. Seal edges and cut several slits in top.

BAKE in preheated 425°F oven 30 minutes or until crust is golden brown. Let stand 5 minutes before serving.

► **MAKES 8 SERVINGS**

Poultry Seasoning

flavor addition

■ **TURKEY OR CHICKEN POT PIE WITH BISCUITS**
Spoon turkey or chicken mixture into 2-quart baking dish. Substitute 1 can (7½ ounces) refrigerated biscuits for the pie crust. Bake in preheated 375°F oven 15 minutes or until biscuits are golden brown.

Meat Loaf

PREP TIME: 10 minutes · COOK TIME: 1 hour

1 tablespoon butter
½ cup finely chopped onion
1 can (8 ounces) tomato sauce
1½ teaspoons **Italian Seasoning,** divided
2 pounds ground beef
2 slices white bread, crumbled
½ cup milk
2 eggs, beaten
2 teaspoons **Season-All® Seasoned Salt**
¾ teaspoon **Ground Black Pepper**

MELT butter in small skillet on medium heat. Add onion; cook and stir 5 minutes or until softened. Cool slightly. Mix tomato sauce and ½ teaspoon of the Italian Seasoning. Set aside.

MIX ground beef, crumbled bread, onion, milk, eggs, Season-All Seasoned Salt, remaining 1 teaspoon Italian Seasoning and Ground Black Pepper in large bowl. Shape into a loaf. Place in foil-lined 13x9-inch baking dish.

BAKE in preheated 375°F oven 45 minutes. Spoon seasoned tomato sauce over meat loaf. Bake 15 minutes longer or until cooked through. Let stand 5 minutes before slicing.

► **MAKES 8 SERVINGS**

Black Peppercorns

flavor variations

■ CLASSIC MEAT LOAF
Prepare as directed. Use 1 cup ketchup in place of the seasoned tomato sauce.

■ MAKE IT EASY
Try **Meat Loaf Seasoning Mix.**

flavor addition

■ MEAT LOAF WITH GRAVY
Prepare as directed. Omit seasoned tomato sauce and serve Meat Loaf with prepared **Brown Gravy Mix.**

Better Burgers

PREP TIME: 5 minutes · COOK TIME: 12 minutes

1 pound ground beef
¼ cup chopped onion
1 teaspoon **Season-All® Seasoned Salt**
¼ teaspoon **Garlic Powder**
¼ teaspoon **Ground Black Pepper**
1 teaspoon Worcestershire sauce
4 slices Cheddar <u>or</u> American cheese
  (optional)
4 hamburger rolls
Lettuce, tomatoes and condiments (optional)

MIX ground beef, onion, Season-All Seasoned Salt, Garlic Powder, Ground Black Pepper and Worcestershire sauce in large bowl. Shape into 4 patties.

BROIL or grill on medium heat 4 to 6 minutes per side or until burgers are cooked through (internal temperature should be 160°F). Add cheese slices to burgers 1 minute before cooking is completed, if desired. Toast rolls on the grill, open-side down, about 30 seconds.

SERVE burgers on toasted rolls. Garnish with desired toppings and condiments.

► MAKES 4 SERVINGS

Fiesta Tacos

PREP TIME: 10 minutes · COOK TIME: 10 minutes

1 pound ground beef <u>or</u> turkey
1 package **Taco Seasoning Mix**
¾ cup water
12 taco shells
Assorted toppings such as shredded lettuce,
  chopped tomatoes and shredded cheese

BROWN ground beef in large skillet on medium-high heat. Drain fat.

STIR in Taco Seasoning Mix and water. Bring to boil. Reduce heat to low; simmer 5 minutes, stirring occasionally.

SPOON into warmed taco shells. Serve with assorted toppings.

► **MAKES 6 SERVINGS**

Sloppy Joe Pizza

PREP TIME: 10 minutes · COOK TIME: 30 minutes

1 pound ground beef
1 package **Sloppy Joe Seasoning Mix**
1 can (6 ounces) tomato paste
1 cup water
1 cup frozen corn, thawed
1 prepared pizza crust (12-inch)
2 cups shredded Colby-Jack cheese
Sliced green onions (optional)

BROWN ground beef in large skillet on medium-high heat. Drain fat. Stir in Sloppy Joe Seasoning Mix, tomato paste and water. Bring to boil. Reduce heat to low; simmer 10 minutes, stirring occasionally. Stir in corn.

PLACE pizza crust on baking sheet. Spoon Sloppy Joe mixture evenly over crust. Sprinkle with cheese.

BAKE in preheated 425°F oven 12 to 15 minutes or until cheese is melted. Sprinkle with green onions, if desired.

► MAKES 8 SERVINGS

flavor variations

■ CHILI PIZZA
Prepare as directed. Substitute **Chili Seasoning Mix** for the Sloppy Joe Seasoning Mix and use shredded Cheddar cheese.

■ TACO PIZZA
Prepare as directed. Substitute **Taco Seasoning Mix** for the Sloppy Joe Seasoning Mix and use shredded Mexican cheese blend.

Stove-Top Tamale Pie

PREP TIME: 10 minutes · COOK TIME: 30 minutes

1½ pounds ground beef
2 packages **Taco Seasoning Mix**
2 cans (8 ounces <u>each</u>) tomato sauce
1 can (16 ounces) kidney beans, undrained
1 package (8 ounces) corn muffin mix
1 cup shredded Cheddar cheese
¼ cup sliced green onions

BROWN ground beef in large skillet on medium-high heat. Drain fat.

STIR in Taco Seasoning Mix, tomato sauce and beans. Bring to boil. Reduce heat to low; cover and simmer 10 minutes.

PREPARE corn muffin mix as directed on package while beef mixture simmers. Drop small spoonfuls of batter over beef mixture. Cover.

COOK on medium-low heat 15 minutes or until corn bread is cooked through. Sprinkle with cheese and green onions. Cover. Cook on low heat until cheese is melted.

► **MAKES 6 SERVINGS**

Taco Casserole

PREP TIME: 10 minutes · COOK TIME: 20 minutes

1½ pounds ground beef <u>or</u> ground turkey
1 package **Taco Seasoning Mix**
1 can (16 ounces) pinto beans, drained and rinsed
1 can (15 ounces) tomato sauce
1 can (11 ounces) Mexican-style corn <u>or</u> whole kernel corn, drained
1 cup shredded Cheddar cheese
1 cup coarsely crushed tortilla chips
Assorted toppings such as sour cream, sliced green onions, shredded lettuce and chopped tomatoes

BROWN ground beef in large skillet on medium-high heat. Drain fat.

STIR in Taco Seasoning Mix, beans, tomato sauce and corn. Bring to boil. Reduce heat to low; simmer 5 minutes, stirring occasionally. Spoon into 2-quart baking dish. Sprinkle with cheese and tortilla chips.

BAKE in preheated 400°F oven 5 to 10 minutes or until cheese is melted. Serve with assorted toppings.

▶ **MAKES 6 SERVINGS**

Touchdown Chili

PREP TIME: 5 minutes · COOK TIME: 15 minutes

1 pound ground beef
1 cup chopped onion
1 package **Chili Seasoning Mix**
1 can (15 ounces) kidney beans, drained
1 can (14½ ounces) diced tomatoes,
    undrained
1 can (8 ounces) tomato sauce
Shredded cheese, sour cream
    and chopped onion (optional)

COOK ground beef and onion in large skillet on medium-high heat 5 minutes, stirring occasionally. Drain fat.

STIR in Chili Seasoning Mix and remaining ingredients. Bring to boil. Reduce heat to low; cover and simmer 10 minutes, stirring occasionally.

SERVE with shredded cheese, sour cream and chopped onion, if desired.

► MAKES 5 SERVINGS

flavor variations

■ ALL-AMERICAN CHILI
Prepare as directed. Use 2 tablespoons **Chili Powder**, 2 teaspoons **Ground Cumin**, 1½ teaspoons **Garlic Salt** and ½ teaspoon **Oregano Leaves** in place of the Chili Seasoning Mix. Simmer 20 minutes.

■ CINCINNATI-STYLE CHILI
Prepare Touchdown or All-American Chili as directed, adding 1 teaspoon **Ground Cinnamon** with Chili Seasoning Mix or spices. Serve over spaghetti. Top with shredded Cheddar cheese and chopped onions, if desired.

Orange Sesame Beef Stir-Fry

PREP TIME: 15 minutes · MARINATE: 15 minutes · COOK TIME: 15 minutes

1 cup orange juice
¼ cup soy sauce
1½ teaspoons **Ground Ginger**
1 teaspoon **Garlic Powder**
¼ teaspoon **Ground Red Pepper**
1 pound boneless beef sirloin steak, cut into thin strips
1 tablespoon oil
4 teaspoons **Sesame Seed,** toasted, divided (see Flavor Tip page 63, for toasting directions)
8 cups fresh vegetables such as broccoli florets, sugar snap peas, sliced onion and red bell pepper strips
1 tablespoon cornstarch
1 tablespoon sugar

MIX orange juice, soy sauce, Ground Ginger, Garlic Powder and Ground Red Pepper in small bowl. Place beef in large resealable plastic bag or glass dish. Reserve ½ of the marinade. Pour remaining marinade over beef. Refrigerate 15 minutes or longer for extra flavor.

HEAT oil in large skillet on high heat. Add beef and 3 teaspoons of the toasted Sesame Seed; stir fry 3 minutes or until beef is no longer pink. Remove beef from skillet. Add vegetables; stir fry 3 to 5 minutes or until tender-crisp.

MIX reserved marinade with cornstarch and sugar. Add to skillet. Stirring constantly, bring to boil on medium heat and boil 1 minute. Return beef to skillet. Cook until heated through. Sprinkle with remaining 1 teaspoon toasted Sesame Seed. Serve over rice, if desired.

► **MAKES 6 SERVINGS**

flavor variation

■ ORANGE SESAME CHICKEN STIR-FRY
Prepare as directed. Use 1 pound boneless skinless chicken breasts, cut into thin strips, in place of the steak.

Ginger

Sesame Steak

PREP TIME: 10 minutes · MARINATE: 30 minutes · COOK TIME: 16 minutes

¼ cup soy sauce
1 tablespoon oil
1 tablespoon brown sugar
1 tablespoon **Sesame Seed,** toasted
1 teaspoon **Onion Powder**
¼ teaspoon **Ground Black Pepper**
¼ teaspoon **Garlic Salt**
¼ teaspoon **Ground Ginger**
1½ pounds boneless beef sirloin steak

MIX soy sauce, oil, brown sugar, toasted Sesame Seed, Onion Powder, Ground Black Pepper, Garlic Salt and Ground Ginger in small bowl. Place steak in large resealable plastic bag or glass dish. Add marinade; turn to coat well.

REFRIGERATE 30 minutes or longer for extra flavor. Remove steak from marinade. Discard any remaining marinade.

BROIL on high or grill over medium-high heat 6 to 8 minutes per side or until desired doneness.

► **MAKES 6 SERVINGS**

Sesame Seed

flavor tip

■ HOW TO TOAST SESAME SEED
Heat a small skillet on medium heat. Add **Sesame Seed;** cook and stir about 2 minutes or until fragrant and golden brown. Immediately pour out of hot pan to avoid over-toasting.

flavor variation

■ SESAME CHICKEN
Prepare as directed. Use 2 pounds boneless skinless chicken breast halves <u>or</u> thighs in place of the steak.

Weeknight Pepper Steak

PREP TIME: 15 minutes · **COOK TIME:** 12 minutes

1 package **Brown Gravy Mix**
¾ cup cold water
1 tablespoon soy sauce
¼ teaspoon **Ground Red Pepper**
1 tablespoon oil
1 pound boneless beef sirloin <u>or</u> flank steak,
  cut into thin strips
1 small onion, cut into thin wedges
1 medium green <u>or</u> red bell pepper
  (<u>or</u> ½ of each), cut into thin strips

MIX Brown Gravy Mix, water, soy sauce and Ground Red Pepper until well blended.

HEAT oil in large skillet on medium-high heat. Add steak; cook and stir 2 minutes or until no longer pink. Stir in Gravy mixture, onion and bell pepper.

BRING to boil. Reduce heat to low; simmer 6 to 8 minutes or until sauce is thickened, stirring occasionally. Serve over rice, if desired.

► **MAKES 4 SERVINGS**

Easy Beef Stew

PREP TIME: 10 minutes · COOK TIME: 20 minutes

2 pounds boneless beef sirloin steak, cut into 1-inch cubes
3 tablespoons flour
2 tablespoons oil
1 package **Beef Stew Seasoning Mix**
3 cups water
1 bag (**24 ounces**) frozen vegetables for stew **or** 5 cups assorted cut-up fresh vegetables

COAT steak cubes with flour. Heat oil in large skillet or Dutch oven on medium-high heat. Add ½ the steak cubes; brown on all sides. Remove from pan and drain. Repeat with remaining steak cubes. Return steak cubes to skillet.

STIR Beef Stew Seasoning Mix and water into skillet. Add vegetables; bring to boil. Reduce heat to low; cover and simmer 15 minutes or until vegetables are tender.

► **MAKES 8 SERVINGS**

flavor variations

■ CLASSIC BEEF STEW
Prepare as directed. Substitute 1 can (14 ounces) beef broth, 2 teaspoons **Season-All® Seasoned Salt,** ½ teaspoon **Thyme Leaves** and ¼ teaspoon **Ground Black Pepper** for the Beef Stew Seasoning Mix and water.

■ MAKE IT EVEN EASIER
Try **Slow Cookers Hearty Beef Stew Seasoning.**

Savory Slow-Cooker Pot Roast

PREP TIME: 10 minutes · COOK TIME: 8 hours on LOW or 4 hours on HIGH

3 pounds boneless beef chuck or rump
  bottom round roast, well-trimmed
5 cups cut-up fresh vegetables such as
  carrots, celery, onions and potatoes
1 package **Slow Cookers Savory Pot
  Roast Seasoning**
1 cup red wine or water

PLACE roast and vegetables in slow cooker.

MIX Savory Pot Roast Seasoning and red wine until blended. Pour over roast and vegetables. Cover.

COOK 8 hours on LOW or 4 hours on HIGH. Remove roast and vegetables to serving platter. Stir sauce before serving.

► MAKES 8 SERVINGS

flavor tip

For best results, do not remove cover during cooking.

flavor variations

■ BEEF BRISKET WITH VEGETABLES
Prepare as directed. Use 1 boneless beef brisket (about 3½ pounds).

■ BEEF BRISKET WITH BEER
Prepare as directed. Use 1 boneless beef brisket (about 3½ pounds). Substitute 1 large onion, cut into wedges, for the vegetables. Use 1 cup beer in place of the red wine. Mix ¼ cup chili sauce and 2 tablespoons brown sugar with the Seasoning Mix and beer.

Herbed Roast Beef

PREP TIME: 10 minutes · COOK TIME: 1½ hours

1 eye round roast (about 3 pounds)
1 tablespoon oil
1 tablespoon **Onion Powder**
2 teaspoons **Garlic Salt**
1½ teaspoons **Italian Seasoning**
½ teaspoon **Coarse Ground Black Pepper**

Perfect Brown Gravy (see recipe below)

PLACE roast on rack in foil-lined roasting pan. Brush lightly with oil.

MIX Onion Powder, Garlic Salt, Italian Seasoning and Coarse Ground Black Pepper in small bowl. Rub evenly over entire roast.

ROAST in preheated 325°F oven 1½ hours or until desired doneness. Cover loosely with foil. Let stand 10 to 15 minutes before slicing. Serve with Perfect Brown Gravy, if desired.

► MAKES 12 SERVINGS

flavor variation

■ ROSEMARY-THYME ROAST BEEF
Substitute 1 teaspoon **Rosemary Leaves** and ½ teaspoon **Thyme Leaves** for the Italian Seasoning.

flavor addition

■ PERFECT BROWN GRAVY
Mix ¼ cup drippings from roasting pan and 1¾ cups water in medium saucepan. Stir in 2 packages **Brown Gravy Mix** until well blended and smooth. Stirring frequently, cook on medium heat until gravy comes to boil. Reduce heat to low; simmer 1 minute or until slightly thickened. (Gravy will thicken upon standing.)

Homestyle Pork Chops

PREP TIME: 10 minutes · COOK TIME: 8 minutes

1 teaspoon **Paprika**
½ teaspoon **Thyme Leaves**
½ teaspoon salt
¼ teaspoon **Ground Black Pepper**
4 bone-in pork chops (about ½ inch thick)
1 tablespoon olive oil

MIX Paprika, Thyme Leaves, salt and Ground Black Pepper in small bowl. Sprinkle evenly over both sides of pork chops.

HEAT oil in large nonstick skillet on medium heat. Add pork chops; cook 4 minutes per side or until desired doneness.

► MAKES 4 SERVINGS

Roast Pork Tenderloin with Ginger Peach Glaze

PREP TIME: 5 minutes · COOK TIME: 45 minutes

1½ teaspoons **Season-All® Seasoned Salt**
1 teaspoon **Ground Thyme**
2 pork tenderloins (about 1 pound each)
½ cup peach <u>or</u> apricot preserves
2 teaspoons Worcestershire sauce
¾ teaspoon **Ground Ginger**

MIX Season-All Seasoned Salt and Ground Thyme in small bowl. Rub evenly over pork. Place on rack in foil-lined roasting pan.

ROAST in preheated 375°F oven 40 to 45 minutes or until desired doneness.

MIX preserves, Worcestershire sauce and Ground Ginger in small bowl. Spoon over pork during the last 10 minutes of cooking.

► **MAKES 8 SERVINGS**

Savory Sage Pork Roast with Apple Pork Gravy

PREP TIME: 10 minutes · COOK TIME: 1¼ hours

2½ teaspoons **Rubbed Sage**
1½ teaspoons **Garlic Salt**
1 teaspoon **Ground Ginger**
½ teaspoon **Ground Black Pepper**
1 boneless center-cut pork roast
  (about 3 pounds)
1 tablespoon oil
2 cups apple juice
2 packages **Pork Gravy Mix**

MIX Rubbed Sage, Garlic Salt, Ground Ginger and Ground Black Pepper in small bowl. Place roast in foil-lined roasting pan with fat side down. Brush entire surface with oil. Rub Seasoning mixture evenly over roast. Pour apple juice into pan.

ROAST in preheated 350°F oven 1¼ hours or until desired doneness, basting with pan juices every 20 minutes. Transfer pork to cutting board. Cover loosely with foil. Let stand 15 minutes before slicing.

MIX ⅔ cup pan juices and 1⅓ cups water (or enough liquid to measure 2 cups) in medium saucepan. Stir in Pork Gravy Mix. Stirring frequently, cook on medium heat until gravy comes to boil. Reduce heat to low; simmer 1 minute or until slightly thickened. (Gravy will thicken more upon standing.) Serve with pork roast.

► **MAKES 12 SERVINGS**

Sage

BBQ Pulled Pork

PREP TIME: 10 minutes · COOK TIME: 8 hours on LOW or 4 hours on HIGH

3 pounds boneless pork shoulder roast, well-trimmed
1 package **Slow Cookers BBQ Pulled Pork Seasoning**
½ cup ketchup
½ cup firmly packed brown sugar
⅓ cup cider vinegar
10 sandwich rolls

PLACE pork in slow cooker. Mix BBQ Pulled Pork Seasoning Mix, ketchup, brown sugar and vinegar until blended. Pour over pork. Cover.

COOK 8 hours on LOW or 4 hours on HIGH. Remove pork from slow cooker.

SHRED pork, using 2 forks. Return pork to slow cooker. Mix and heat with sauce before serving. Serve on sandwich rolls with Summertime Slaw (see recipe on page 95), if desired.

► MAKES 10 SERVINGS

flavor tip

For best results, do not remove cover during cooking.

flavor variation

■ BBQ PULLED CHICKEN
Prepare as directed. Use 2½ pounds boneless skinless chicken breasts in place of the pork roast. Stir in ½ cup water with the cider vinegar. Cook 5 hours on LOW or 2½ hours on HIGH.

■ BBQ PULLED BEEF
Prepare as directed. Use 3½ pounds boneless chuck roast, trimmed and cut into pieces, in place of the pork roast. Substitute 1 can (6 ounces) tomato paste for the ketchup and add ½ cup water.

Baked Crusted Salmon

PREP TIME: 5 minutes · COOK TIME: 10 minutes

1 teaspoon **Onion Powder**
1 teaspoon **Season-All® Seasoned Salt**
½ teaspoon **Dill Weed**
Oil
4 salmon fillets (about 1 pound)

MIX Onion Powder, Season-All Seasoned Salt and Dill Weed in small bowl.

PLACE fish, skin-side down, in lightly greased baking dish. Lightly brush with oil. Sprinkle seasoning mixture evenly over fish.

BAKE in preheated 450°F oven 8 to 10 minutes or until fish flakes easily with a fork.

► **MAKES 4 SERVINGS**

flavor variation

■ OLD BAY BAKED CRUSTED SALMON
Use **OLD BAY® Seasoning** in place of the Season-All Seasoned Salt and only ½ teaspoon **Onion Powder.**

Dill Weed

Short-Cut Paella

PREP TIME: 10 minutes · COOK TIME: 30 minutes

1 tablespoon olive oil
½ pound smoked sausage <u>or</u> chorizo, cut in
   half lengthwise and then into ¼-inch slices
½ cup chopped onion
1 cup long-grain rice, uncooked
2 teaspoons **Italian Seasoning**
½ teaspoon **Ground Turmeric**
2 cups chicken broth
1 can (14½ ounces) diced tomatoes, drained
1 pound large shrimp, peeled and deveined
1 cup frozen peas
Black Peppercorn Grinder (optional)

HEAT oil in large skillet on medium heat. Add sausage and onion; cook and stir 3 minutes or until onion is softened. Add rice, Italian Seasoning and Ground Turmeric; cook and stir 2 minutes.

STIR in broth. Bring to boil. Reduce heat to low; cover and simmer 15 minutes. Stir in tomatoes. Place shrimp in single layer on top of rice; top with peas. Cover.

COOK on medium-low heat 8 to 10 minutes or until rice is tender and shrimp turn pink. Season to taste with Black Peppercorn Grinder, if desired.

► **MAKES 6 SERVINGS**

Ground Turmeric

flavor variation
■ Use ¼ teaspoon **Saffron,** crumbled, in place of the Ground Turmeric.

OLD BAY Crab Cakes

PREP TIME: 10 minutes · COOK TIME: 10 minutes

2 slices white bread, crusts removed and crumbled
2 tablespoons mayonnaise
2 teaspoons OLD BAY® Seasoning
2 teaspoons Parsley Flakes
½ teaspoon prepared yellow mustard
1 egg, beaten
1 pound fresh lump crabmeat

MIX bread, mayonnaise, OLD BAY Seasoning, Parsley Flakes, mustard and egg in large bowl until well blended. Gently stir in crabmeat. Shape into 4 patties.

BROIL 10 minutes without turning or fry until golden brown on both sides. Sprinkle with additional OLD BAY Seasoning before serving, if desired.

► **MAKES 4 SERVINGS**

Tilapia with Savory Herb Butter

PREP TIME: 10 minutes · COOK TIME: 8 minutes

½ teaspoon salt
¼ teaspoon **Ground Black Pepper**
4 tilapia fillets (about 1 pound)
4 tablespoons Savory Herb Butter

SAVORY HERB BUTTER:
½ cup (1 stick) butter, softened
1 teaspoon **Garlic Powder**
1 teaspoon **Ground Mustard**
1 teaspoon **Italian Seasoning**

SPRINKLE salt and Ground Black Pepper evenly on both sides of fish. Place fish on broiler pan.

BROIL 8 minutes or until fish flakes easily with a fork.

MEANWHILE prepare Savory Herb Butter: mix butter, Garlic Powder, Ground Mustard, and Italian Seasoning in a small bowl until well blended and smooth. (Can be made up to 1 week ahead; store in the refrigerator until needed.)

SPREAD 1 tablespoon of the Savory Herb Butter on each fish fillet before serving.

► MAKES 4 SERVINGS

flavor variations

■ GRILLED HERBED TILAPIA
Place 1 fish fillet in center of each sheet of heavy-duty aluminum foil. Season with **Black Peppercorn** and **Sea Salt Grinders**, if desired. Top each fillet with 1 tablespoon of the Savory Herb Butter. Bring up foil sides; double fold top and ends to tightly seal packet. Grill over medium-high heat 10 to 12 minutes or until fish flakes easily with a fork, turning once.

■ GRILLED SALMON AND PEPPERS
Place 1 salmon fillet (about 4 ounces) on each sheet of heavy-duty aluminum foil. Season with **Black Peppercorn** and **Sea Salt Grinders,** if desired. Top each with 1 tablespoon of the Savory Herb Butter and ⅓ cup green, red and yellow bell pepper strips. Bring up foil sides; double fold top and ends to tightly seal packet. Grill over medium-high heat 15 minutes or until fish flakes easily with a fork, turning once.

Pasta Primavera

PREP TIME: 15 minutes · COOK TIME: 15 minutes

8 ounces linguine pasta
4½ cups assorted vegetables, such as
   broccoli florets, sliced carrots, red bell
   pepper strips and peas
½ cup chicken broth
¼ cup dry white wine
1 teaspoon **Dill Weed**
1 teaspoon **Garlic Salt**
¼ teaspoon **Thyme Leaves**
1 cup heavy cream
½ cup grated Parmesan cheese
2 tablespoons butter

COOK pasta in large saucepan as directed on package, adding vegetables during last 3 to 4 minutes of cooking. Drain well.

PLACE broth, wine, Dill Weed, Garlic Salt, Thyme Leaves, cream, Parmesan cheese and butter in same saucepan. Bring to boil, stirring constantly with wire whisk. Reduce heat to low; simmer 5 minutes. Add pasta and vegetables; toss gently to coat well. Serve with additional grated Parmesan cheese, if desired.

► **MAKES 6 SERVINGS**

Thyme

flavor variation

■ SHRIMP PASTA PRIMAVERA
Prepare as directed. Add 1 pound large shrimp, peeled and deveined, to pasta with vegetables during last 3 minutes of cooking.

Easy Cheese Lasagna

PREP TIME: 15 minutes · COOK TIME: 1 hour

2 containers (15 ounces <u>each</u>) ricotta cheese
2 cups shredded mozzarella cheese, divided
2 eggs, beaten
1 tablespoon **California Style® Wet Garlic**
1 teaspoon **Italian Seasoning**
1 teaspoon **Parsley Flakes**
½ teaspoon salt
¼ teaspoon **Ground Black Pepper**
1 jar (26 ounces) spaghetti sauce
½ cup water
9 uncooked lasagna noodles
¼ cup grated Parmesan cheese

MIX ricotta cheese, 1½ cups of the mozzarella cheese, eggs, California Style Wet Garlic, Italian Seasoning, Parsley Flakes, salt and Ground Black Pepper in large bowl until well blended. Pour spaghetti sauce into medium bowl. Pour water into empty spaghetti-sauce jar; cover and shake well. Add to spaghetti sauce; mix well.

SPREAD about 1 cup of the sauce on the bottom of 13x9-inch baking dish. Top with 3 of the lasagna noodles. Spread ½ of the cheese mixture over noodles. Repeat sauce, noodles and cheese layer once. Top with remaining noodles and sauce, making sure to cover noodles completely with sauce. Sprinkle with remaining ½ cup mozzarella cheese and Parmesan cheese. Cover with foil.

BAKE in preheated 350°F oven 45 minutes. Remove foil. Bake 15 minutes longer or until noodles are tender. Let stand 15 minutes before cutting. Serve with additional spaghetti sauce, if desired.

► MAKES 12 SERVINGS

Parsley

flavor variations

■ Substitute 1 teaspoon **Garlic Powder** for the California Style Wet Garlic.

■ SPINACH LASAGNA
Prepare as directed. Mix 2 packages (10 ounces <u>each</u>) frozen chopped spinach, thawed and squeezed dry, into the ricotta cheese mixture.

  COOKING WITH FLAVOR

Chunky Tomato Sauce

PREP TIME: 5 minutes · COOK TIME: 25 minutes

1 can (14½ ounces) diced
  tomatoes, undrained
1 can (6 ounces) tomato paste
¾ cup water
1 tablespoon **Italian Seasoning**
2 teaspoons sugar
1 teaspoon **Garlic Powder**
½ teaspoon **Onion Salt**

MIX tomatoes, tomato paste, water, Italian Seasoning, sugar, Garlic Powder and Onion Salt in large saucepan. Bring to boil on medium-high heat. Reduce heat to low; simmer 20 minutes, stirring occasionally.

SERVE over pasta.

► MAKES 5 SERVINGS

flavor variations

■ Substitute 1 teaspoon each **Basil Leaves** and **Oregano Leaves** for the Italian Seasoning.

■ CHUNKY TOMATO AND MUSHROOM SAUCE
Heat 1 tablespoon olive oil in large saucepan on high heat. Add 1 package (8 ounces) sliced mushrooms; cook and stir 5 minutes or until lightly browned. Stir in remaining ingredients and cook as directed.

Garlic

Side Dishes & Salads

This selection of appealing vegetables, **pleasing** potatoes and grains and **well-dressed** salads will make every mealtime even more enjoyable.

Herbed Asparagus

PREP TIME: 10 minutes · COOK TIME: 5 minutes

1 pound asparagus, ends trimmed
1 teaspoon **Parsley Flakes**
½ teaspoon **Basil Leaves**
⅛ teaspoon **Ground Black Pepper**
3 tablespoons butter, melted
2 plum tomatoes, seeded and chopped
2 tablespoons shredded Parmesan cheese

COOK asparagus 5 minutes or until tender-crisp. Drain well. Place on serving dish.

STIR Parsley Flakes, Basil Leaves and Ground Black Pepper into melted butter.

POUR butter mixture over hot asparagus. Sprinkle with chopped tomatoes and Parmesan cheese.

► MAKES 4 SERVINGS

flavor variations

■ SPRING THYME ASPARAGUS
Prepare as directed. Use ½ teaspoon **Garlic Powder** and ¼ teaspoon **Thyme Leaves** in place of the Parsley Flakes and Basil Leaves. Omit tomatoes and Parmesan cheese.

■ LEMON HERB ASPARAGUS
Cook and drain 1½ pounds asparagus as directed. Mix butter with 1 teaspoon **Basil Leaves** and ½ teaspoon <u>each</u> grated lemon peel <u>and</u> **Oregano Leaves.** Pour over hot asparagus. Makes 6 servings.

■ HERBED GREEN BEANS
Substitute an equal amount of fresh green beans, washed and stem ends snapped off, for the asparagus in the above recipes.

Three-Seed Green Beans and Tomatoes

PREP TIME: 10 minutes · COOK TIME: 15 minutes

1 bag (12 ounces) trimmed green beans <u>or</u>
   wax beans (<u>or</u> a combination), cut in half
1 tablespoon olive oil
2 large cloves garlic, thinly sliced
½ teaspoon **Cumin Seed**
½ teaspoon **Mustard Seed**
¼ teaspoon **Fennel Seed**
⅛ teaspoon **Crushed Red Pepper**
1 pint grape tomatoes, halved
¼ teaspoon salt

BRING ½ inch water to boil in large skillet on high heat. Add beans; cover and cook 7 to 9 minutes or until tender-crisp, stirring occasionally. Drain well. Set aside.

MIX oil, garlic, Cumin Seed, Mustard Seed, Fennel Seed and Crushed Red Pepper in same skillet. Cook and stir on medium heat 2 minutes or until seeds are fragrant. Add tomatoes and salt; toss to coat well.

COOK and stir 2 minutes or until tomatoes start to soften. Add beans; cook and stir 2 minutes longer or until heated through.

► **MAKES 6 SERVINGS**

flavor variations

■ BASIL GREEN BEANS
Prepare as directed. Use ½ teaspoon
Basil Leaves in place of the Cumin
Seed, Mustard Seed, Fennel Seed and
Crushed Red Pepper; add with the
tomatoes.

■ ITALIAN GREEN BEANS
Prepared as directed. Use ½ teaspoon
Italian Seasoning in place of the
Cumin Seed, Mustard Seed and Fennel
Seed; add with the tomatoes.

Mustard Seed

Stir-Fry Vegetables

PREP TIME: 15 minutes · COOK TIME: 10 minutes

¼ cup water
1 tablespoon soy sauce
1 teaspoon **Garlic Powder**
1 teaspoon **Ground Ginger**
¼ teaspoon **Crushed Red Pepper**
1 teaspoon cornstarch
2 tablespoons oil, divided
1 medium onion, sliced thin
1 cup diagonally sliced carrots
2 cups broccoli florets
2 cups sugar snap peas
1 large red bell pepper, cut into strips
2 teaspoons **Sesame Seed**, toasted

MIX water, soy sauce, Garlic Powder, Ground Ginger and Crushed Red Pepper in small bowl. Stir in cornstarch until smooth. Set aside.

HEAT 1 tablespoon of the oil in wok or large deep skillet on medium-high heat. Add onion and carrots; stir-fry 2 minutes. Add remaining 1 tablespoon oil and remaining vegetables; stir fry 5 to 7 minutes or until vegetables are tender-crisp.

RESTIR soy sauce mixture. Stir into skillet. Stirring constantly, bring to boil on medium heat and boil 1 minute. Sprinkle with Sesame Seed before serving. Serve over rice, if desired.

▶ **MAKES 10 SERVINGS**

Sesame Seed

flavor variation

■ TWO-SEED STIR FRY
Use **Black Sesame Seed** or a combination of both Sesame Seeds for visual appeal.

flavor tip

■ HOW TO TOAST SESAME SEED
Heat a small skillet on medium heat. Add **Sesame Seed**; cook and stir about 2 minutes or until fragrant and golden brown. Immediately pour out of hot pan to avoid over-toasting.

Roasted Vegetables

PREP TIME: 15 minutes · COOK TIME: 30 minutes

2 tablespoons oil
1 teaspoon **Garlic Salt**
1 teaspoon **Italian Seasoning**
6 cups assorted cut-up fresh vegetables
  such as bell peppers, onions, carrots,
  asparagus, zucchini and yellow squash

MIX oil, Garlic Salt and Italian Seasoning in large bowl. Add vegetables; toss to coat well.

SPREAD in single layer on foil-lined 15x10x1-inch baking pan.

BAKE in preheated 450°F oven 30 minutes or until vegetables are tender, stirring occasionally.

► MAKES 6 SERVINGS

flavor variations

■ FENNEL ROASTED VEGETABLES
Prepare as directed. Mix ½ teaspoon **Fennel Seed** into the seasoning mixture.

■ HARVEST ROASTED VEGETABLES
Prepare as directed. Use 1 teaspoon each **Season-All® Seasoned Salt** and **Rubbed Sage** and ¼ teaspoon **Ground Black Pepper** in place of the Garlic Salt and Italian Seasoning. For the vegetables, use 2 cups each red potato wedges, baby carrots and onion wedges.

Chili-Roasted Potato Wedges

PREP TIME: 10 minutes · COOK TIME: 30 minutes

2 pounds baking potatoes
2 tablespoons olive oil
1 teaspoon **Chili Powder**
1 teaspoon kosher salt

CUT potatoes into 3x½-inch wedges. Place in large bowl. Add oil; toss to coat well.

MIX Chili Powder and salt. Sprinkle over potatoes; toss to coat evenly. Arrange potatoes in single layer on foil-lined 15x10x1-inch baking sheet.

BAKE in preheated 450°F oven 30 minutes or until potatoes are tender and golden brown.

► **MAKES 6 SERVINGS**

flavor variations

■ BAKED SWEET POTATO FRIES
Cut 2 peeled sweet potatoes into ¼-inch sticks. Place on baking sheet sprayed with nonstick cooking spray. Toss with 1½ teaspoons **Season-All® Seasoned Salt**. Arrange in single layer in pan. Spray with additional nonstick cooking spray. Bake in preheated 400°F oven 30 minutes, turning fries after 15 minutes. Makes 4 servings.

■ EASY ROASTED POTATOES
Mix 1 tablespoon olive oil, 1 teaspoon each **Dill Weed** and **Garlic Powder**, ½ teaspoon salt and ¼ teaspoon **Coarse Ground Black Pepper** in large bowl. Add 2 pounds red potatoes, cut into wedges; toss to coat well. Spread in single layer on foil-lined 15x10x1-inch baking sheet. Bake in preheated 400°F oven 40 minutes or until potatoes are tender and golden brown. Makes 6 servings.

Chili Powder

Garlic Mashed Potatoes

PREP TIME: 15 minutes · COOK TIME: 10 minutes

2 pounds russet <u>or</u> Idaho potatoes, peeled
  and quartered
1 teaspoon **California Style® Wet Garlic**
1 teaspoon salt
½ cup milk
¼ cup (½ stick) butter, cut into chunks
½ cup shredded Cheddar cheese
1 teaspoon **Parsley Flakes**

PLACE potatoes in 2-quart saucepan. Cover with water. Bring to boil. Reduce heat to low; cover and simmer 10 minutes or until potatoes are tender.

DRAIN well. Return potatoes to saucepan. Add California Style Wet Garlic and salt.

MASH with potato masher, gradually adding milk and then butter. Stir in cheese and Parsley Flakes.

► **MAKES 6 SERVINGS**

Parsley

flavor variations

■ Substitute ½ teaspoon **Garlic Powder** for the California Style Crushed Wet Garlic.

■ ALMOST-INSTANT
GARLIC MASHED POTATOES
Stir 1 teaspoon **California Style Wet Garlic** into 4 cups hot prepared (instant <u>or</u> refrigerated) mashed potatoes. Mix in ½ cup shredded Cheddar cheese, if desired.

Parmesan Rice Pilaf

PREP TIME: 5 minutes · **COOK TIME:** 25 minutes

2 tablespoons butter
1 cup rice
2 cups chicken broth
½ teaspoon **Garlic Powder**
½ teaspoon **Parsley Flakes**
¼ teaspoon **Ground Black Pepper**
2 tablespoons grated Parmesan cheese
2 tablespoons toasted sliced almonds

MELT butter in medium saucepan on medium heat. Add rice; cook and stir 3 minutes. Stir in chicken broth, Garlic Powder, Parsley Flakes and Ground Black Pepper.

BRING to boil. Reduce heat to low; cover and simmer 20 minutes or until rice is tender. Remove from heat.

STIR in Parmesan cheese and almonds.

► **MAKES 4 SERVINGS**

flavor variations

■ **PARMESAN PILAF WITH BACON AND PEAS**
Prepare as directed. Stir 1 cup frozen peas and 3 slices cooked and crumbled bacon into rice mixture during last 5 minutes of cooking.

■ **CURRIED PILAF**
Prepare as directed. Omit Parmesan cheese. Add ½ teaspoon **Curry Powder** with spices. Stir 1 cup shredded carrots and ¼ cup raisins into rice mixture during last 5 minutes of cooking.

Black Peppercorns

Rice with Asparagus, Mushrooms and Toasted Sesame Seed

PREP TIME: 10 minutes · COOK TIME: 30 minutes

1 cup Arborio rice
3 tablespoons **Sesame Seed**
2 tablespoons olive oil
2 cloves garlic, minced
1 package (8 ounces) sliced cremini <u>or</u> baby portobello mushrooms
½ pound asparagus, ends trimmed and cut into 1-inch pieces
½ cup grated Parmesan cheese
½ teaspoon salt

BRING 6 cups water to boil in large saucepan. Add rice; return to boil. Reduce heat to medium; cook, uncovered, 12 to 15 minutes or until rice is tender with a little bite in the center, stirring occasionally. Drain rice, reserving 1 cup of the liquid. Return rice to saucepan. Cover to keep warm.

HEAT large skillet on medium-high heat. Add Sesame Seed; cook and stir 3 minutes or until golden. Immediately pour out of hot skillet to avoid over-toasting.

HEAT oil in same skillet. Add garlic; cook and stir on medium heat about 1 minute. Add mushrooms; cook and stir 5 minutes or until lightly browned and tender. Add asparagus; cook and stir 3 to 4 minutes or until tender-crisp.

STIR vegetables, toasted Sesame Seed, Parmesan cheese and salt into rice. Stir in reserved liquid, ¼ cup at a time, until desired creaminess.

► MAKES 4 SERVINGS

Savory Orzo

PREP TIME: 10 minutes · COOK TIME: 20 minutes

1½ cups orzo pasta
4 slices bacon
1 cup sliced green onions
½ cup grated Parmesan cheese, divided
½ cup pine nuts, toasted
2 teaspoons **Italian Seasoning**
¾ teaspoon **Season-All® Seasoned Salt**

COOK orzo as directed on package. Drain well. Set aside.

COOK bacon in large skillet on medium-high heat until crisp. Drain bacon on paper towels and crumble. Drain drippings, reserving 2 tablespoons. Return drippings to same skillet. Add green onions; cook and stir 1 to 2 minutes or until tender-crisp.

STIR in orzo, bacon, ¼ cup of the Parmesan cheese, pine nuts, Italian Seasoning and Season-All Seasoned Salt. Cook 1 to 2 minutes or until heated through. Sprinkle with remaining ¼ cup Parmesan cheese. See photo, page 44.

► MAKES 6 SERVINGS

Field Greens with Oranges, Strawberries and Vanilla Vinaigrette

PREP TIME: 20 minutes

⅓ cup olive oil
3 tablespoons white wine vinegar
1 teaspoon **Pure Vanilla Extract**
½ teaspoon salt
½ teaspoon sugar
¼ teaspoon **Ground Black Pepper**
1 package (6 ounces) field greens <u>or</u> baby spinach
2 seedless oranges, peeled and sectioned
2 cups strawberry halves <u>or</u> slices
½ cup toasted pecan pieces

MIX oil, vinegar, Pure Vanilla Extract, salt, sugar and Ground Black Pepper in small bowl with wire whisk until well blended.

TOSS greens with oranges, strawberries and pecans in large bowl. (Or divide among individual serving plates.) Serve with vinaigrette.

► **MAKES 6 SERVINGS**

Black Peppercorns

flavor variation

■ TARRAGON VINAIGRETTE
Prepare as directed. Omit Pure Vanilla Extract. Stir 1 teaspoon **Tarragon Leaves** into the vinaigrette.

Creamy Pepper Dressing

PREP TIME: 5 minutes

¼ cup mayonnaise
¼ cup sour cream
2 tablespoons milk
2 teaspoons cider vinegar
1 teaspoon **Coarse Ground Black Pepper**
¼ teaspoon **Garlic Powder**
¼ teaspoon **Onion Salt**

MIX mayonnaise, sour cream, milk, vinegar, Ground Black Pepper, Garlic Powder and Onion Salt in medium bowl until well blended. Cover.

REFRIGERATE until ready to serve. Stir dressing before serving.

► MAKES 4 SERVINGS

Caesar Salad

PREP TIME: 10 minutes

½ cup mayonnaise
¼ cup shredded Parmesan cheese
2 tablespoons lemon juice
1 tablespoon **California Style® Wet Garlic**
1 to 2 anchovy fillets, mashed
½ teaspoon Dijon mustard
½ teaspoon Worcestershire sauce
1 tablespoon milk
1 package (10 ounces) Romaine lettuce
1 cup croutons

MIX mayonnaise, Parmesan cheese, lemon juice, California Style Wet Garlic, mashed anchovy fillets, mustard and Worcestershire sauce in small bowl until well blended. Stir in milk. Refrigerate until ready to serve.

TOSS lettuce and croutons in large bowl. Add dressing; toss to coat well. Serve with additional Parmesan cheese, if desired.

► MAKES 5 SERVINGS

flavor variations

■ CHICKEN or SHRIMP CAESAR SALAD
Prepare as directed. Top with grilled chicken or shrimp to serve as a main dish salad.

Garlic

Summertime Slaw

PREP TIME: 5 minutes · REFRIGERATE: 2 hours

1 cup mayonnaise
2 tablespoons sugar
2 tablespoons cider vinegar
1 teaspoon **Celery Seed**
1 teaspoon **Ground Mustard**
1 teaspoon **Season-All® Seasoned Salt**
1 package (16 ounces) shredded coleslaw
   mix

MIX mayonnaise, sugar, vinegar, Celery Seed, Ground Mustard and Season-All Seasoned Salt in large bowl. Add coleslaw mix; toss to coat well. Cover.

REFRIGERATE 2 hours or until ready to serve. Stir before serving.

► MAKES 8 SERVINGS

flavor variations

■ Use ¼ cup sour cream in place of ¼ cup of the mayonnaise.

■ FAR EAST SUMMER SLAW
Prepare as directed. Omit Celery Seed and Ground Mustard. Use rice wine vinegar in place of the cider vinegar. Stir ½ teaspoon **Ground Ginger** and ⅛ teaspoon **Ground Red Pepper** into the mayonnaise mixture.

■ VANILLA SLAW
Prepare as directed. Omit Celery Seed and Ground Mustard. Stir ½ teaspoon **Pure Vanilla Extract** into the mayonnaise mixture.

■ SERVING SUGGESTION
Summertime Slaw makes a delicious accompaniment to BBQ Pulled Pork (see recipe on page 71).

Easy Layered Salad

PREP TIME: 20 minutes · REFRIGERATE: 1 hour

4 cups mixed salad greens
2 tomatoes, chopped (about 2 cups)
2 cups shredded Cheddar cheese, divided
1 cup frozen peas, thawed
3 hard-cooked eggs, sliced
2 cups cubed cooked ham
½ cup chopped red onion
½ cup mayonnaise
½ cup sour cream
1 teaspoon **Dill Weed**
½ teaspoon **Ground Mustard**

PLACE salad greens in large serving bowl. Layer tomatoes, 1 cup of the cheese, peas, eggs, ham and onion over greens.

MIX mayonnaise, sour cream, Dill Weed and Ground Mustard in medium bowl until well blended. Spread evenly over salad. Cover.

REFRIGERATE at least 1 hour or overnight until ready to serve. Sprinkle with remaining 1 cup cheese just before serving.

► **MAKES 12 SERVINGS**

Ground Mustard

flavor variations

■ SUPREME LAYERED SALAD
Prepare as directed. Use 1½ teaspoons **Salad Supreme® Seasoning** in place of the Dill Weed and Ground Mustard.

■ MAKE IT YOUR WAY
Use any variety of your favorite ingredients such as cooked chicken or turkey, canned tuna, olives, canned beans, cooked potatoes, cooked green beans, sliced mushrooms, corn or crumbled cooked bacon in this salad.

Cool Cucumber Salad

PREP TIME: 10 minutes · REFRIGERATE: 1 hour

2 cups thinly sliced cucumbers (4 small <u>or</u> 2 large cucumbers)
½ teaspoon salt
1 cup thinly sliced red onion
¼ cup vinegar
¼ cup water
1 tablespoon sugar
½ teaspoon **Dill Weed**
¼ teaspoon **Coarse Grind Black Pepper**
Pinch **Ground Red Pepper**

PLACE cucumber slices in medium bowl. Sprinkle with salt. Stir in onions.

MIX vinegar, water, sugar, Dill Weed, Coarse Grind Black Pepper and Ground Red Pepper in small bowl. Pour over cucumber mixture; toss lightly. Cover.

REFRIGERATE 1 hour or until ready to serve. Toss before serving.

▶ MAKES 6 SERVINGS

Dill Weed

flavor variation

■ SOUR CREAM DILL CUCUMBER SALAD
Prepare cucumbers and onion as directed. Omit vinegar, water and sugar. Mix ½ cup sour cream with Dill Weed, Coarse Grind Black Pepper and Ground Red Pepper with wire whisk in small bowl until well blended. Toss with cucumber mixture.

Classic Potato Salad

PREP TIME: 15 minutes · COOK TIME: 10 minutes

5 cups cubed potatoes (about 3 pounds)
⅓ cup mayonnaise
⅓ cup sour cream
¼ cup chopped celery
¼ cup sliced green onions
1½ teaspoons **Mustard Seed**
1½ teaspoons **Season-All® Seasoned Salt**

BRING potatoes to boil in lightly salted water in large saucepan. Cook 10 minutes or until potatoes are fork-tender. Drain well. Cool slightly.

MIX mayonnaise, sour cream, celery, green onions, Mustard Seed and Season-All Seasoned Salt in large bowl. Add potatoes; gently toss to coat.

SERVE immediately or refrigerate until ready to serve.

► **MAKES 6 SERVINGS**

flavor variation

■ DILLY POTATO SALAD
Prepare as directed. Stir 1 teaspoon **Dill Weed** into mayonnaise mixture.

Mustard Seed

Two Potato Salad with Toasted Pecans

PREP TIME: 25 minutes · **COOK TIME:** 10 minutes

1 pound russet potatoes, peeled and cubed
1 pound sweet potatoes, peeled and cubed
½ cup oil
½ teaspoon grated lime peel
2 tablespoons lime juice
2 tablespoons cider vinegar
1 tablespoon brown sugar
1 teaspoon **Ground Ginger**
½ teaspoon salt
¼ teaspoon **Ground Nutmeg**
1 cup thinly sliced celery
½ cup chopped red onion
½ cup toasted chopped pecans

BRING potatoes to boil in lightly salted water in large saucepan. Cook 10 minutes or until potatoes are fork-tender. (Do not overcook.) Drain well. Cool slightly.

MIX oil, lime peel, lime juice, vinegar, sugar, Ground Ginger, salt and Ground Nutmeg in large bowl until well blended. Add potatoes; toss to coat well. Gently stir in celery, onion and pecans.

SERVE immediately or refrigerate until ready to serve.

► **MAKES 8 SERVINGS**

Supreme Pasta Salad

PREP TIME: 15 minutes · COOK TIME: 15 minutes

8 ounces pasta
1 cup Italian salad dressing
2 tablespoons **Salad Supreme® Seasoning**
3 cups assorted vegetables such as broccoli
   flowerets, sliced carrots and cherry
   tomatoes halves
½ cup chopped red onion

COOK pasta as directed on package. Rinse under cold water; drain well.

PLACE pasta in large bowl. Add dressing, Salad Supreme Seasoning, vegetables and onion; toss gently. Cover.

REFRIGERATE until ready to serve. Toss lightly before serving.

► **MAKES 8 SERVINGS**

flavor variations

■ SUPREME PASTA SALAD
WITH SALAD TOPPINS
Prepare as directed. Mix ½ cup **Salad
Toppins™** into pasta mixture. Sprinkle
with additional ¼ cup **Salad Toppins**
just before serving.

■ ANTIPASTO SUPREME PASTA SALAD
Prepare as directed. Mix 1 cup <u>each</u>
bite-size mozzarella cheese balls <u>and</u>
sliced salami pieces into pasta mixture.

Grilling

Grilling makes everything look **beautiful** and taste **delicious** . . .

and these fired-up favorites are no exception!

Beer Can Chicken

PREP TIME: 7 minutes · COOK TIME: 55 minutes

1 whole chicken (about 4 pounds)
1 tablespoon olive oil
¼ cup **Grill Mates® Montreal Chicken Seasoning,** divided
1 can (12 ounces) beer

PREHEAT gas grill to medium heat (325°F to 350°F). Remove giblets from chicken cavity. Rinse chicken inside and out; pat dry. Rub chicken with oil. Rub cavity with 1 tablespoon of the Montreal Chicken Seasoning. Sprinkle remaining Montreal Chicken Seasoning evenly over chicken.

POUR out about 2 ounces beer and poke 2 holes in top of can. Hold chicken upright (legs pointing down) and insert opened beer can into cavity. Stand chicken in upright position in center of grill. Position legs to best support chicken (similar to a tripod). Close lid.

GRILL 55 minutes or until chicken is cooked through. Remove chicken from can before serving.

► **MAKES 8 SERVINGS**

---

flavor addition

■ GRILLED CORN ON THE COB
Pull back husks from corn cobs without detaching. Remove silk. Spread 1 tablespoon Savory Herb Butter (see recipe on page 75) onto each ear of corn. Rewrap husks around corn. Grill over medium heat, turning frequently, 20 minutes or until corn is tender.

Lemon Rosemary Grilled Chicken

PREP TIME: 5 minutes · MARINATE: 30 minutes · COOK TIME: 16 minutes

¼ cup olive oil
2 tablespoons lemon juice
1 teaspoon **Garlic Powder**
1 teaspoon **Onion Salt**
1 teaspoon **Rosemary Leaves,** crushed
1 pound boneless skinless chicken breast
  halves

MIX oil, lemon juice, Garlic Powder, Onion Salt and Rosemary Leaves in small bowl. Place chicken in large resealable plastic bag or glass dish. Add marinade; turn to coat well.

REFRIGERATE 30 minutes or longer for extra flavor. Remove chicken from marinade. Discard any remaining marinade.

GRILL over medium-high heat 6 to 8 minutes per side or until chicken is cooked through, turning frequently.

► MAKES 4 SERVINGS

Zesty Herb Citrus Chicken

PREP TIME: 10 minutes · MARINATE: 15 minutes · COOK TIME: 16 minutes

1 package **Grill Mates® Zesty Herb** or
  Garlic, Herb & Wine Marinade
1 teaspoon finely grated lemon, lime or
  orange peel
¼ cup lemon, lime or orange juice
¼ cup oil
¼ cup water
2 pounds boneless skinless chicken breast
  halves or thighs

MIX Marinade Mix, lemon peel, lemon juice, oil and water in small bowl. Place chicken in large resealable plastic bag or glass dish. Add marinade; turn to coat well.

REFRIGERATE 15 minutes or longer for extra flavor. Remove chicken from marinade. Discard any remaining marinade.

GRILL over medium-high heat 6 to 8 minutes per side or until chicken is cooked through, turning frequently.

► MAKES 8 SERVINGS

flavor variation

■ TO PREPARE WITH BONE-IN CHICKEN
Use 2½ pounds chicken parts in place of the boneless chicken. With lid closed, grill over medium heat 30 to 40 minutes or until chicken is cooked through.

Montreal Turkey Burgers

PREP TIME: 10 minutes · COOK TIME: 12 minutes

1 pound ground turkey
1 tablespoon **Grill Mates® Montreal Chicken Seasoning**
4 hamburger rolls
Lettuce, tomato and condiments

MIX ground turkey and Chicken Seasoning in medium bowl until well blended. Shape into 4 patties.

GRILL over medium heat 4 to 6 minutes per side or until burgers are cooked through (internal temperature reaches 160°F). Toast rolls on the grill, open side down, about 30 seconds, or until golden.

SERVE burgers on toasted rolls. Garnish with desired toppings and condiments.

► **MAKES 4 SERVINGS**

All-American Burgers

PREP TIME: 10 minutes · COOK TIME: 12 minutes

1 pound ground beef
¼ cup ketchup
1 tablespoon **Grill Mates® Hamburger Seasoning**
1 teaspoon Worcestershire sauce
4 slices Cheddar <u>or</u> American cheese
4 hamburger rolls
8 slices cooked bacon (optional)
Lettuce, tomato and condiments

MIX ground beef, ketchup, Hamburger Seasoning and Worcestershire sauce in large bowl. Shape into 4 patties.

GRILL over medium heat 4 to 6 minutes per side or until burgers are cooked through (internal temperature reaches 160°F). Add cheese slices to burgers 1 minute before cooking is completed. Toast rolls on the grill, open side down, about 30 seconds, or until golden.

SERVE burgers on toasted rolls with bacon slices, if desired. Garnish with desired toppings and condiments.

► **MAKES 4 SERVINGS**

Montreal Peppered Steak

PREP TIME: 5 minutes · MARINATE: 30 minutes · COOK TIME: 16 minutes

½ **cup olive oil**
¼ **cup soy sauce**
4 **teaspoons Grill Mates® Montreal Steak**
Seasoning
2 **pounds boneless beef sirloin or New York**
strip steaks

MIX oil, soy sauce and Montreal Steak Seasoning in small bowl. Place steak in large resealable plastic bag or glass dish. Add marinade; turn to coat well.

REFRIGERATE 30 minutes or longer for extra flavor. Remove steak from marinade. Discard any remaining marinade.

GRILL over medium-high heat 6 to 8 minutes per side for medium-rare, or to desired doneness.

► **MAKES 8 SERVINGS**

Cuban-Style Marinated Steak

PREP TIME: 5 minutes · MARINATE: 30 minutes · COOK TIME: 16 minutes

¼ cup orange juice
2 tablespoons fresh lime juice
2 tablespoons oil
2 tablespoons **Grill Mates® Montreal Steak Seasoning**
1½ teaspoons **Oregano Leaves**
½ teaspoon **Ground Cumin**
1½ pounds boneless beef sirloin steak

MIX orange juice, lime juice, oil, Montreal Steak Seasoning, Oregano Leaves and Ground Cumin in small bowl. Place steak in large resealable plastic bag or glass dish. Add marinade; turn to coat well.

REFRIGERATE 30 minutes or longer for extra flavor. Remove steak from marinade. Discard any remaining marinade.

GRILL over medium-high heat 6 to 8 minutes per side for medium-rare or to desired doneness.

► MAKES 6 SERVINGS

Spice-Rubbed Pork Chops with Summertime Salsa

PREP TIME: 15 minutes · COOK TIME: 14 minutes

¼ cup orange juice
2 teaspoons chopped fresh mint
1 teaspoon balsamic vinegar
½ teaspoon **Ground Cinnamon**
2 peaches <u>or</u> 3 nectarines, peeled, seeded and cut into small cubes (2 cups)
3 tablespoons **Grill Mates® Pork Rub**
6 boneless pork chops (1-inch thick)
1 cup fresh raspberries

MIX orange juice, mint, vinegar and Ground Cinnamon in medium bowl. Add peaches; toss to coat well. Set aside.

RUB Pork Rub evenly on both sides of each pork chop.

GRILL over medium heat 5 to 7 minutes per side or until desired doneness. Gently toss raspberries with peach mixture. Serve with pork chops.

► MAKES 6 SERVINGS

flavor variations

■ Use 1 can (15 ounces) sliced peaches, drained and chopped, and ¼ cup frozen raspberries, thawed, in place of the fresh fruit. Use only 1 tablespoon of the orange juice.

Ground Cinnamon

Mesquite Glazed Sausage

PREP TIME: 15 minutes · MARINATE: 30 minutes · COOK TIME: 20 minutes

1 package **Grill Mates® Mesquite Marinade**
⅓ cup orange juice
¼ cup orange marmalade
2 tablespoons water
½ teaspoon **Curry Powder**
1¼ pounds mild Italian sausage links

COOK and stir Marinade Mix and orange juice in small saucepan on medium heat until smooth. Add marmalade, water and Curry Powder; stirring constantly, bring to boil. Reduce heat to low; simmer 1 minute. Remove from heat; cool completely.

PIERCE sausages with fork. Place in large resealable plastic bag or glass dish. Add ½ of the glaze; turn to coat evenly. Refrigerate 30 minutes or longer for extra flavor. Remove sausages from marinade. Discard any remaining marinade.

GRILL sausages over medium heat 20 minutes or until cooked through, turning occasionally and brushing with remaining glaze.

► MAKES 5 SERVINGS

Honey Ginger Grilled Salmon

PREP TIME: 5 minutes · MARINATE: 15 minutes · COOK TIME: 16 minutes

⅓ cup orange juice
⅓ cup soy sauce
¼ cup honey
1 teaspoon **Ground Ginger**
1 teaspoon **Garlic Powder**
1 green onion, chopped
4 salmon fillets (about 1½ pounds)

MIX orange juice, soy sauce, honey, Ground Ginger, Garlic Powder and green onion in small bowl until well blended. Place salmon in large resealable plastic bag or glass dish. Add marinade; turn to coat well.

REFRIGERATE 15 minutes or longer for extra flavor. Remove salmon from marinade. Discard any remaining marinade.

GRILL over medium-high heat 6 to 8 minutes per side or until fish flakes easily with a fork.

► **MAKES 4 SERVINGS**

BBQ Potatoes

PREP TIME: 10 minutes · **COOK TIME:** 35 minutes

4 medium red potatoes, cut into
¾-inch cubes
1 tablespoon oil
2 tablespoons **Grill Mates® Barbecue
Seasoning**
1 large onion, cut into thin wedges

TOSS potatoes with oil in large bowl. Add Barbecue Seasoning; toss to coat evenly.

PLACE potatoes on large wide sheet of heavy-duty aluminum foil. Place onions evenly on top of potatoes. Bring up foil sides; double fold top and ends to tightly seal packet.

GRILL over medium-high heat 30 to 35 minutes or until potatoes are tender, turning packet halfway through cooking time.

► **MAKES 8 SERVINGS**

Mixed Vegetable Grill

PREP TIME: 15 minutes · **COOK TIME:** 12 minutes

2 tablespoons light brown sugar
1½ teaspoons **Basil Leaves**
1½ teaspoons **Garlic Salt**
½ teaspoon **Season-All® Seasoned Salt**
⅛ teaspoon **Ground Red Pepper**
2 tablespoons olive oil
8 asparagus spears, ends trimmed
1 medium red <u>or</u> yellow bell pepper, cut
   lengthwise into 6 strips
1 medium zucchini, cut lengthwise into
   ½-inch slices
1 medium yellow squash, cut lengthwise into
   ½-inch slices
1 small sweet potato, cut into ¼-inch rounds
1 small red onion, cut into ½-inch rounds

MIX brown sugar, Basil Leaves, Garlic Salt, Season-All Seasoned Salt and Ground Red Pepper in small bowl. Drizzle oil over vegetables in large bowl; toss to coat well. Add Seasoning mixture; toss to coat well.

PLACE vegetables in grill basket or grill rack, or thread onto skewers.

GRILL over medium heat 10 to 12 minutes or until vegetables are tender, turning occasionally.

► **MAKES 6 SERVINGS**

Desserts

Looking for an afternoon **indulgence**, a **mouthwatering** meal-ender, or a **tantalizing** take-along? We've got a number of **tempting** treats that will satisfy everyone's sweet tooth.

Lemon Clove Cookies

PREP TIME: 15 minutes · **REFRIGERATE:** 1 hour · **COOK TIME:** 15 minutes per batch

2 cups flour
¼ teaspoon **Ground Cloves**
⅛ teaspoon salt
¾ cup (1½ sticks) butter, softened
1 cup sugar
1 egg
½ teaspoon **Pure Lemon Extract**

Lemon Glaze (optional)

MIX flour, Ground Cloves and salt in medium bowl; set aside.

BEAT butter and sugar in large bowl with electric mixer on medium speed until light and fluffy. Add egg and Pure Lemon Extract; beat until well blended. Stir in flour mixture. Divide dough in half. Form each half into a log about 1½ inches in diameter and 9 inches long. Wrap in wax paper.

REFRIGERATE 1 hour or until firm. Cut dough into ¼-inch-thick slices. Place 2 inches apart on ungreased baking sheets.

BAKE in preheated 350°F oven 12 to 15 minutes or until lightly browned. Cool on baking sheets 1 minute. Remove to wire racks; cool completely. Drizzle with Lemon Glaze (see recipe below), if desired.

► **MAKES 5 DOZEN**

flavor addition

■ **LEMON GLAZE**
Mix 1½ cups confectioners' sugar, 2 tablespoons plus 1 teaspoon water and ¼ teaspoon **Pure Lemon Extract** in small bowl. Drizzle glaze over cooled cookies. Let stand until set.

Ground Cloves

Gingersnap Cookies

PREP TIME: 15 minutes · **COOK TIME:** 12 minutes per batch

2 cups flour
2 teaspoons baking soda
½ teaspoon salt
1 tablespoon **Ground Ginger**
1 teaspoon **Ground Cinnamon**
¾ cup shortening
1 cup sugar
¼ cup molasses
1 egg
Additional sugar for rolling

MIX flour, baking soda, salt, Ground Ginger and Ground Cinnamon in medium bowl; set aside.

BEAT shortening and sugar in large bowl with electric mixer on medium speed until light and fluffy. Beat in molasses and egg. Gradually stir in flour mixture until well mixed.

SHAPE dough into 1-inch balls. Roll in additional sugar. Place 2 inches apart on ungreased baking sheets.

BAKE in preheated 350°F oven 12 minutes. Cool on baking sheets 1 minute. Remove to wire racks; cool completely.

► **MAKES 4 DOZEN**

Vanilla Sugar Cookies

PREP TIME: 30 minutes · **REFRIGERATE:** 2 hours · **COOK TIME:** 8 minutes per batch

1 cup (2 sticks) butter, softened
1½ cups sugar
2 teaspoons **Cream of Tartar**
1 teaspoon baking soda
¼ teaspoon salt
2 eggs
1 teaspoon **Pure Vanilla Extract**
2¾ cups flour
Additional sugar for rolling

BEAT butter in large bowl with electric mixer on medium speed until light and fluffy. Add 1½ cups sugar, Cream of Tartar, baking soda and salt; beat until well blended, scraping side of bowl occasionally. Beat in eggs and Pure Vanilla Extract. Gradually stir in flour until well mixed.

REFRIGERATE dough about 2 hours or until firm. Shape dough into 1-inch balls. Roll in additional sugar. Place 2 inches apart on ungreased baking sheets.

BAKE in preheated 400°F oven 6 to 8 minutes or until lightly browned. Cool on baking sheets 1 minute. Remove to wire racks; cool completely.

► **MAKES 5 DOZEN**

flavor variations

■ **ALMOND SUGAR COOKIES**
Prepare as directed. Use 1 teaspoon **Pure Almond Extract** in place of the Pure Vanilla Extract.

■ **LEMON SUGAR COOKIES**
Prepare as directed. Use 1 teaspoon **Pure Lemon Extract** in place of the Pure Vanilla Extract.

■ **SNICKERDOODLES**
Prepare as directed. Mix ½ teaspoon **Ground Cinnamon** into the 1½ cups sugar. Roll unbaked cookie dough balls in a mixture of ¼ cup sugar and 1 tablespoon **Ground Cinnamon.**

Twice as Nice Almond Cookies

PREP TIME: 15 minutes · **COOK TIME:** 9 minutes per batch

1 package (15 ounces) sugar cookie mix
½ teaspoon **Pure Almond Extract**
1 cup chopped sliced almonds

PREPARE cookie mix as directed on package, stirring in Pure Almond Extract.

SHAPE dough into balls. Roll in almonds. Place 2 inches apart on ungreased baking sheets.

BAKE and cool as directed on package.

► **MAKES 3 DOZEN**

flavor addition

■ COZY CINNAMON COCOA
Stir ½ teaspoon **Pure Vanilla Extract** and a dash **Ground Cinnamon** into 1 cup prepared hot chocolate until well blended. Use a **Cinnamon Stick** as a stirrer.

Almond

Almond White Chocolate Chunk Cookies

PREP TIME: 15 minutes · **COOK TIME:** 10 minutes per batch

2¼ cups flour
1 teaspoon baking soda
½ teaspoon salt
1 cup (2 sticks) butter, softened
1½ cups sugar
2 eggs
1½ teaspoons **Pure Almond Extract**
8 ounces white baking chocolate, coarsely
   chopped
1⅓ cups slivered almonds

MIX flour, baking soda and salt in medium bowl; set aside.

BEAT butter and sugar in large bowl with electric mixer on medium speed until light and fluffy. Add eggs and Pure Almond Extract; beat until well blended. Gradually beat in flour mixture until well mixed. Stir in chocolate and almonds. Drop by heaping tablespoonfuls 2 inches apart onto ungreased baking sheets.

BAKE in preheated 375°F oven 10 minutes or until edges are lightly browned. Cool on baking sheets 1 minute. Remove to wire racks; cool completely.

► **MAKES 6 DOZEN**

flavor variations

■ **MACADAMIA AND CRANBERRY WHITE CHOCOLATE CHUNK COOKIES**
Prepare as directed. Use 1½ teaspoons **Pure Vanilla Extract** in place of the Pure Almond Extract. Use 1⅓ cups chopped macadamia nuts in place of the slivered almonds and add 1 cup dried cranberries.

■ **WALNUT CHOCOLATE CHUNK COOKIES**
Prepare as directed. Use 1½ teaspoons **Pure Vanilla Extract** in place of the Pure Almond Extract. Use 8 ounces semi-sweet baking chocolate in place of the white chocolate and 1⅓ cups chopped walnuts in place of the almonds.

Lemon Cheesecake Bars

PREP TIME: 15 minutes · **COOK TIME:** 45 minutes · **REFRIGERATE:** 4 hours

1½ cups graham cracker crumbs
⅓ cup butter, melted
½ teaspoon **Ground Ginger**
3 packages (8 ounces <u>each</u>) cream cheese,
  softened
1 cup sugar
¼ cup milk
2 tablespoons flour
1½ teaspoons **Pure Lemon Extract**
1 teaspoon **Pure Vanilla Extract**
3 eggs

MIX graham cracker crumbs, butter and Ground Ginger. Press firmly onto bottom of foil-lined 13x9-inch baking pan. Refrigerate until ready to use.

BEAT cream cheese and sugar in large bowl with electric mixer on medium speed until well blended. Add milk, flour, Pure Lemon Extract and Pure Vanilla Extract; mix well. Add eggs, 1 at a time, beating on low speed after each addition just until blended. Pour over crust.

BAKE in preheated 350°F oven 40 to 45 minutes or until center is almost set. Cool completely on wire rack.

REFRIGERATE 4 hours or overnight. Lift out of pan onto cutting board. Cut into bars. Garnish with Berry Topping (see recipe below), if desired. Store leftover bars in the refrigerator.

► **MAKES 24 SERVINGS**

flavor addition

■ BERRY TOPPING
Garnish tops of bars with assorted berries such as blackberries, blueberries, sliced strawberries and raspberries. Melt 3 tablespoons currant <u>or</u> apple jelly, let cool slightly and brush over berries.

flavor variations

■ ORANGE CHEESECAKE BARS
Prepare as directed. Use 1½ teaspoons **Pure Orange Extract** in place of the Pure Lemon Extract.

■ RASPBERRY CHEESECAKE BARS
Prepare as directed. Use 2 teaspoons **Raspberry Extract** in place of the Pure Lemon Extract.

Orange-Kissed Brownies

PREP TIME: 5 minutes · **COOK TIME:** 30 minutes

1 package (21 ounces) fudge brownie mix
1 tablespoon **Pure Orange Extract**
1 cup semi-sweet chocolate chips

ORANGE-KISSED CHOCOLATE FROSTING:
1 can (16 ounces) ready-to-spread
 chocolate frosting
1 teaspoon **Pure Orange Extract**

Oranges, sliced and cut into wedges,
 for garnish (optional)

PREPARE brownie mix as directed on package. Stir in 1 tablespoon Pure Orange Extract and chocolate chips.

BAKE and cool as directed on package.

MIX frosting and 1 teaspoon Pure Orange Extract until well blended. Spread evenly over brownies. Cut into squares. Garnish with sliced oranges, if desired.

▶ **MAKES 2 DOZEN**

flavor variations

■ RASPBERRY-KISSED BROWNIES
Prepare as directed. Omit Pure Orange Extract. Add 4 teaspoons **Raspberry Extract** to the brownie mix and 2 teaspoons **Raspberry Extract** to the frosting.

■ MEXICAN CHOCOLATE BROWNIES
Prepare as directed. Omit Pure Orange Extract. Add 1 tablespoon **Pure Vanilla Extract** and 1 teaspoon **Ground Cinnamon** to the brownie mix. Add ¼ teaspoon **Ground Cinnamon** to the frosting.

Easy Chocolate Fondue

PREP TIME: 5 minutes

⅔ cup light corn syrup
½ cup heavy cream
1 teaspoon **Pure Vanilla Extract**
1 package (8 ounces) semi-sweet baking
   chocolate

MICROWAVE corn syrup, cream and Pure Vanilla Extract in large microwavable bowl on HIGH 1½ minutes or until mixture comes to boil. Add chocolate; stir until chocolate is completely melted and mixture is smooth.

SERVE warm as a dip with assorted cookies, pretzels, cut-up fresh fruit and pound cake or angel food cake cubes.

► **MAKES 2 CUPS**

flavor variations

■ EASY CHOCOLATE RASPBERRY FONDUE
Prepare as directed. Use 1 teaspoon
Raspberry Extract in place of the
Pure Vanilla Extract.

■ EASY CHOCOLATE ORANGE FONDUE
Prepare as directed. Use 1 teaspoon
Pure Orange Extract in place of the
Pure Vanilla Extract.

■ EASY CHOCOLATE ALMOND FONDUE
Prepare as directed. Use ½ teaspoon
Pure Almond Extract in place of the
Pure Vanilla Extract.

■ EASY MEXICAN CHOCOLATE FONDUE
Prepare as directed. Add 1 teaspoon
Ground Cinnamon <u>or</u> 1 teaspoon <u>each</u>
Ground Cinnamon <u>and</u> **Chili Powder**
with the chocolate.

Easy Molten Cakes

PREP TIME: 15 minutes · **COOK TIME:** 14 minutes

4 ounces semi-sweet baking chocolate
½ cup (1 stick) butter
1 teaspoon **Pure Vanilla Extract**
1 cup confectioners' sugar
2 eggs
1 egg yolk
6 tablespoons flour

RASPBERRY SAUCE (OPTIONAL):
1 package frozen raspberries
½ teaspoon **Raspberry Extract**

BUTTER 6 (6-ounce) custard cups or soufflé dishes. Place on baking sheet.

MICROWAVE chocolate and butter in large microwavable bowl on HIGH 1 minute or until butter is melted. Stir with wire whisk until chocolate is completely melted. Stir in Pure Vanilla Extract. Stir in sugar until well blended. Whisk in eggs and yolk. Stir in flour. Pour batter into prepared custard cups.

BAKE in preheated 425°F oven 10 to 14 minutes or until sides are firm but centers are soft. Let stand 1 minute. Carefully loosen edges with small knife. Invert cakes onto serving plates. Serve immediately. Serve with Raspberry Sauce (see recipe below) or whipped cream, if desired.

MIX 1 package (10 ounces) frozen raspberries in juice, thawed, and ½ teaspoon Raspberry Extract until well blended. Refrigerate until ready to serve.

► **MAKES 6 SERVINGS**

flavor variation

■ ALMOND MOLTEN CAKES
Prepare as directed. Add 1 teaspoon **Pure Almond Extract** with the Pure Vanilla Extract.

■ ORANGE MOLTEN CAKES
Prepare as directed. Add 1 teaspoon **Pure Orange Extract** with the Pure Vanilla Extract.

■ RASPBERRY MOLTEN CAKES
Prepare as directed. Add 4 teaspoons **Raspberry Extract** with the Pure Vanilla Extract.

■ CINNAMON MOLTEN CAKES
Prepare as directed. Add 1 teaspoon **Ground Cinnamon** with the Pure Vanilla Extract.

Triple Chocolate Cake

PREP TIME: 15 minutes · **COOK TIME:** 55 minutes

1 package (18¼ ounces) devil's food cake mix
1 package (4-serving size) chocolate instant
   pudding mix
4 eggs
1¼ cups water
½ cup vegetable oil
1 tablespoon **Pure Vanilla Extract**
1 cup semi-sweet chocolate chips

CHOCOLATE GLAZE:
½ cup sugar
¼ cup milk
3 tablespoons butter
½ cup semi-sweet chocolate chips
1 teaspoon **Pure Vanilla Extract**

BEAT cake mix, pudding mix, eggs, water, oil and Pure Vanilla Extract in large bowl with electric mixer on low speed 30 seconds. Beat on medium speed 2 minutes.

STIR in chocolate chips. Pour into greased and floured 12-cup Bundt pan.

BAKE in preheated 350°F oven 55 minutes or until toothpick inserted in center comes out clean. Cool in pan 10 minutes. Invert cake onto wire rack. Cool completely.

FOR THE GLAZE, mix sugar, milk and butter in small saucepan on medium heat. Stirring constantly on medium heat, bring to boil and boil 1 minute. Remove from heat. Stir in chocolate chips and Pure Vanilla Extract until chips are melted. Drizzle glaze over cooled cake.

► **MAKES 16 SERVINGS**

flavor variations

■ **TRIPLE CHOCOLATE ALMOND CAKE**
Prepare as directed. Use **Pure Almond Extract** in place of the Pure Vanilla Extract. Add 1 teaspoon to the cake mix and ½ teaspoon to the glaze.

■ **TRIPLE CHOCOLATE ORANGE CAKE**
Prepare as directed. Use **Pure Orange Extract** in place of the Pure Vanilla Extract. Add 2 teaspoons to the cake mix and ½ teaspoon to the glaze.

■ **TRIPLE CHOCOLATE PEPPERMINT CAKE**
Prepare as directed. Use **Pure Peppermint Extract** in place of the Pure Vanilla Extract. Add 1 teaspoon to the cake mix and ½ teaspoon to the glaze.

■ **TRIPLE CHOCOLATE RASPBERRY CAKE**
Prepare as directed. Use **Raspberry Extract** in place of the Pure Vanilla Extract. Add 1 tablespoon to the cake and 1 teaspoon to the glaze.

■ **TRIPLE CHOCOLATE CINNAMON CAKE**
Prepare as directed. Add 1 tablespoon **Ground Cinnamon** to the cake mix and ½ teaspoon to the glaze.

Easy Lemon Poppy Seed Cake

PREP TIME: 10 minutes · **COOK TIME:** 45 minutes

1 package (16 ounces) pound cake mix
½ cup sour cream
½ cup water
2 eggs
4 teaspoons **Pure Lemon Extract**
2 tablespoons **Poppy Seed**

BEAT cake mix, sour cream, water, eggs and Pure Lemon Extract in large bowl with electric mixer on low speed just to moisten. Beat on medium speed 3 minutes.

STIR in Poppy Seed until well blended. Pour into greased and floured 10-cup Bundt pan.

BAKE in preheated 350°F oven 40 to 45 minutes or until toothpick inserted in center comes out clean. Cool in pan 10 minutes. Invert cake onto wire rack. Cool completely. Sprinkle with confectioners' sugar or drizzle with Lemon Glaze (see recipe below), if desired.

► **MAKES 12 SERVINGS**

flavor variations

■ **ORANGE POPPY SEED CAKE**
Prepare cake as directed. Use **Pure Orange Extract** in place of the Pure Lemon Extract. Drizzle with Orange Glaze, if desired.

■ **ORANGE GLAZE**
Prepare Lemon Glaze as directed. Use **Pure Orange Extract** in place of the Pure Lemon Extract.

■ **SUNSHINE POPPY SEED CAKE**
Prepare cake as directed. Use 2 teaspoons <u>each</u> **Pure Lemon Extract** <u>and</u> **Pure Orange Extract** in place of the 4 teaspoons Pure Lemon Extract. Drizzle with Lemon <u>or</u> Orange Glaze, if desired.

flavor addition

■ **LEMON GLAZE**
Mix 1½ cups confectioners' sugar, 1 tablespoon water and ½ teaspoon **Pure Lemon Extract** in medium bowl until smooth. If glaze is too thick, stir in additional 1 to 3 teaspoons water until glaze is of desired consistency.

Poppy Seed

Vanilla Cake with Vanilla Buttercream Frosting

PREP TIME: 15 minutes · **COOK TIME:** 35 minutes

2½ cups flour
1 tablespoon baking powder
1 teaspoon salt
1 cup (2 sticks) butter, softened
1½ cups granulated sugar
4 teaspoons Pure Vanilla Extract
4 eggs
¾ cup milk

VANILLA BUTTERCREAM FROSTING:
1 cup (2 sticks) butter, softened
2 teaspoons Pure Vanilla Extract
1 package (16 ounces) confectioners' sugar
2 tablespoons milk

FOR THE CAKE, mix flour, baking powder and salt in large bowl. Set aside. Beat butter in large bowl with electric mixer on medium speed 30 seconds or until softened. Add sugar and Pure Vanilla Extract; beat until light and fluffy, scraping down sides of bowl occasionally. Beat in eggs on medium-low speed just until blended. Alternately beat in flour mixture and milk just until mixed. Pour into greased and floured 13x9-inch baking pan.

BAKE in preheated 350°F oven 30 to 35 minutes or until toothpick inserted in center comes out clean. Cool completely on wire rack.

FOR THE FROSTING, beat butter in large bowl with electric mixer on medium speed until light and fluffy. Add Pure Vanilla Extract; mix well. Gradually beat in confectioners' sugar, beating well after each addition and frequently scraping sides and bottom of bowl. Add milk; beat well. Spread in an even layer over top of cooled cake.

► **MAKES 24 SERVINGS**

Vanilla Rich Chip Cake

PREP TIME: 10 minutes · **COOK TIME:** 50 minutes

1 package (18¼ ounces) yellow cake mix
1 package (4-serving size) vanilla instant
   pudding mix
1 cup sour cream
½ cup vegetable oil
½ cup water
4 eggs
1 tablespoon **Pure Vanilla Extract**
1 cup miniature chocolate chips

BEAT cake mix, pudding mix, sour cream, oil, water, eggs and Pure Vanilla Extract in large bowl with electric mixer on low speed just to moisten. Beat on medium speed 2 minutes.

STIR in chocolate chips. Pour into greased and floured 12-cup Bundt pan.

BAKE in preheated 350°F oven 50 minutes or until toothpick inserted in center comes out clean. Cool in pan 10 minutes. Invert onto wire rack. Cool completely. Sprinkle with confectioners' sugar or drizzle with Vanilla Butter Glaze (see recipe below), if desired.

► **MAKES 16 SERVINGS**

flavor variations

■ **ALMOND RICH CHIP CAKE**
Prepare as directed. Use 1 teaspoon
Pure Almond Extract in place of the
Pure Vanilla Extract.

■ **RASPBERRY RICH CHIP CAKE**
Prepare as directed. Use 4 teaspoons
Raspberry Extract in place of the Pure
Vanilla Extract.

■ **RUM RICH CHIP CAKE**
Prepare as directed. Use 1 tablespoon
Imitation Rum Extract in place of the
Pure Vanilla Extract.

flavor addition

■ **VANILLA BUTTER GLAZE**
Prepare cake as directed. Mix
3 tablespoons melted butter, 2¼ cups
confectioners' sugar, 3 tablespoons water
and 1½ teaspoons **Pure Vanilla Extract**
until smooth. Let glaze stand 3 minutes
or until thickened.

No-Bake Vanilla Cheesecake

PREP TIME: 10 minutes · **REFRIGERATE:** 3 hours

2 packages (8 ounces <u>each</u>) cream cheese, softened
½ cup sugar
1 tablespoon **Pure Vanilla Extract**
1 tub (8 ounces) frozen whipped topping, thawed
1 prepared graham cracker <u>or</u> vanilla crumb crust (6 ounces)
Fresh fruit, for garnish (optional)

BEAT cream cheese, sugar and Pure Vanilla Extract in large bowl with electric mixer on medium speed until well blended and smooth. Gently stir in whipped topping. Spoon into crust.

REFRIGERATE 3 hours or until set. Garnish with fresh fruit or serve with Easy Strawberry Sauce (see recipe below), if desired. Store leftover cheesecake in refrigerator.

► **MAKES 8 SERVINGS**

flavor variations

■ STRAWBERRY NO-BAKE CHEESECAKE
Prepare as directed. Use 2 tablespoons **Imitation Strawberry Extract** in place of the Pure Vanilla Extract.

■ NO-BAKE CHEESECAKE TARTS
Prepare Cheesecake Filling as directed. Use 12 graham cracker tart crusts in place of the crumb crust. Fill each with ⅓ cup filling and refrigerate 3 hours or until filling is set. Makes 12 servings.

flavor variations

■ EASY STRAWBERRY SAUCE
Mix ½ cup strawberry jam and ¼ teaspoon **Pure Vanilla Extract** <u>or</u> **Pure Almond Extract.**

Apple Cardamom Cheesecake

PREP TIME: 30 minutes · **COOK TIME:** 1 hour 10 minutes · **REFRIGERATE:** 4 hours

CRUST:
1½ cups graham cracker crumbs
⅓ cup butter, melted
¼ cup sugar
¾ teaspoon **Ground Cardamom**

GLAZED APPLES:
4 medium apples (about 2 pounds), peeled and cored
¼ cup (½ stick) butter
¼ cup sugar
¾ teaspoon **Ground Cardamom**

FILLING:
2 packages (8 ounces <u>each</u>) cream cheese, softened
⅔ cup sugar
2 teaspoons **Pure Vanilla Extract**
½ teaspoon grated lemon peel
4 eggs

FOR THE CRUST, mix graham cracker crumbs, melted butter, sugar and Ground Cardamom in medium bowl. Press firmly onto bottom and 1 inch up side of 9-inch springform pan; set aside.

FOR THE GLAZED APPLES, cut apples into thin slices (about ¼ inch thick). Place apples, butter, sugar and Ground Cardamom in large skillet. Cook on medium heat 5 to 10 minutes or until apples begin to caramelize, turning frequently. Arrange apples on bottom of crust.

FOR THE FILLING, beat cream cheese in large bowl with electric mixer on medium speed until fluffy. Gradually beat in sugar, Pure Vanilla Extract and lemon peel. Add eggs, 1 at a time, beating on low speed after each addition just until blended. Spoon evenly over apples.

BAKE in preheated 325°F oven 60 to 70 minutes or until center is almost set. Turn oven off and allow cheesecake to cool in oven 1 hour with door slightly ajar. Run small knife or metal spatula around rim of pan to loosen cheesecake; cool before removing rim of pan. Cool in pan on wire rack.

REFRIGERATE 4 hours or overnight.

► **MAKES 12 SERVINGS**

Vanilla Cream in Pastry Shells

PREP TIME: 15 minutes · **COOK TIME:** 15 minutes

1 package (10 ounces) frozen puff pastry shells
½ package (4 ounces) cream cheese, softened
¼ cup sugar
2 teaspoons **Pure Vanilla Extract**
½ cup heavy cream
Fresh berries and mint leaves, for garnish (optional)

PREPARE and bake pastry shells as directed on package. Cool completely.

BEAT cream cheese, sugar and Pure Vanilla Extract in large bowl until smooth and creamy. Whip cream in medium bowl with electric mixer on medium speed until stiff peaks form. Gently stir into cream cheese mixture. Cover.

REFRIGERATE until ready to serve. Fill or pipe cream mixture into pastry shells just before serving. Garnish with fresh berries and mint leaves, if desired.

► **MAKES 6 SERVINGS**

flavor variations

■ ALMOND CREAM IN PASTRY SHELLS
Prepare as directed. Use 1 teaspoon **Pure Almond Extract** in place of the Pure Vanilla Extract.

■ RASPBERRY CREAM IN PASTRY SHELLS
Prepare as directed. Use 2 teaspoons **Raspberry Extract** in place of the Pure Vanilla Extract.

■ CREAM TARTS
Prepare as directed. Use graham cracker tart crusts in place of the puff pastry shells.

Very Vanilla Berry Dessert

PREP TIME: 10 minutes

2 cups halved <u>or</u> sliced strawberries
2 cups blueberries
1 cup raspberries
¾ cup confectioners' sugar, divided
3 teaspoons **Pure Vanilla Extract,** divided
1½ cups heavy cream

MIX berries, ¼ cup of the sugar and 2 teaspoons of the Pure Vanilla Extract in large bowl.

BEAT cream, remaining ½ cup sugar and remaining 1 teaspoon Pure Vanilla Extract in large bowl with electric mixer on medium speed until soft peaks form.

REFRIGERATE both berry mixture and whipped cream until ready to serve. To serve, spoon whipped cream over berries in individual dessert dishes.

► **MAKES 8 SERVINGS**

flavor variations

■ **VERY RASPBERRY BERRY DESSERT**
Prepare as directed. Use **Raspberry Extract** in place of the Pure Vanilla Extract.

■ **VERY BERRY SHORTCAKE**
Prepare as directed. For each shortcake, spoon ½ cup of the berry mixture over 1 slice pound cake. Top each with ¼ cup of the whipped cream. Makes 10 shortcakes.

■ **EASY VERY BERRY TRIFLE**
Prepare as directed. Mix 1 teaspoon **Pure Orange Extract** into cream before whipping. Gently stir ¼ cup sour cream into whipped cream. Layer 2 cups angel food cake cubes, ½ of the berry mixture <u>and</u> ½ of the whipped cream in 2-quart glass serving bowl. Repeat layers. Cover. Refrigerate at least 2 hours before serving. Garnish with additional berries, if desired.

Easy Lemon Mousse

PREP TIME: 10 minutes

½ package (4 ounces) cream cheese, softened
½ cup sugar, divided
1½ cups heavy cream
3 tablespoons lemon juice
1 teaspoon **Pure Lemon Extract**
1 teaspoon **Pure Vanilla Extract**
Lemon slices, fresh berries and mint leaves, for garnish (optional)

BEAT cream cheese and ¼ cup of the sugar in large bowl until smooth and creamy.

BEAT cream, remaining ¼ cup sugar, lemon juice, Pure Lemon Extract and Pure Vanilla Extract in large bowl with electric mixer on medium speed until stiff peaks form. Add ½ of the whipped cream mixture to cream cheese mixture; stir until well blended. Gently stir in remaining whipped cream mixture. Cover.

REFRIGERATE until ready to serve. Spoon or pipe into dessert dishes. Garnish with lemon slices, fresh berries and mint leaves, if desired.

► **MAKES 6 SERVINGS**

Lemon

flavor variation

■ **EASY VANILLA MOUSSE**
Prepare as directed. Use 1 tablespoon **Pure Vanilla Extract** in place of the Pure Lemon Extract and lemon juice.

Apple Pear Crisp

PREP TIME: 20 minutes · **COOK TIME:** 45 minutes

2 apples, peeled, cored and sliced
2 firm ripe pears, peeled, cored and sliced
1 tablespoon lemon juice
½ teaspoon **Pure Vanilla Extract**
2 tablespoons cornstarch
2 teaspoons **Ground Cinnamon**

STREUSEL TOPPING:
½ cup flour
½ cup quick-cooking oats
½ cup firmly packed light brown sugar
1 teaspoon **Ground Cinnamon**
6 tablespoons cold butter, cut into chunks

TOSS apple and pear slices with lemon juice and Pure Vanilla Extract in large bowl. Mix cornstarch and 2 teaspoons Ground Cinnamon in small bowl. Sprinkle over fruit; toss to coat well. Spoon into lightly greased 11x7-inch baking dish.

FOR the Streusel Topping, mix flour, oats, brown sugar and 1 teaspoon Ground Cinnamon in medium bowl. Cut in butter with pastry blender or 2 knives until coarse crumbs form. Sprinkle evenly over fruit.

BAKE in preheated 350°F oven 40 to 45 minutes or until fruit is tender and topping is golden brown. Serve warm with ice cream or whipped cream, if desired.

► **MAKES 6 SERVINGS**

flavor variations

■ SPICED APPLE PEAR CRISP
Prepare as directed. Use **Apple Pie Spice** in place of the Ground Cinnamon. Add 1 teaspoon to the fruit mixture and ½ teaspoon to the Streusel Topping.

■ APPLE CRISP <u>OR</u> PEAR CRISP
Prepare as directed. Use all apples <u>or</u> all pears.

■ PEACH-BLUEBERRY CRISP
Prepare as directed. Use 4 cups peeled sliced peaches and 1 cup blueberries in place of the apples and pears. Increase cornstarch to 3 tablespoons.

■ TRIPLE BERRY CRISP
Prepare as directed. Use 2 cups <u>each</u> blueberries, raspberries <u>and</u> sliced strawberries in place of the apples and pears and increase cornstarch to 3 tablespoons.

Cinnamon Pecan Pie

PREP TIME: 15 minutes · **COOK TIME:** 55 minutes

1 refrigerated pie crust (from 15-ounce package)
3 eggs, slightly beaten
1 cup firmly packed light brown sugar
1 cup light corn syrup
2 tablespoons butter, melted
2 teaspoons **Pure Vanilla Extract**
½ teaspoon **Ground Cinnamon**
1½ cups pecan pieces

PREPARE pie crust as directed on package for 1-crust pie using 9-inch pie plate.

MIX eggs, sugar, corn syrup, butter, Pure Vanilla Extract and Ground Cinnamon in large bowl until blended. Stir in pecans. Pour into crust.

BAKE in preheated 350°F oven 50 to 55 minutes or until edges are set and center is still soft. Cool completely on wire rack. Serve with Cinnamon Whipped Cream (see recipe below), if desired.

▶ **MAKES 8 SERVINGS**

flavor addition

■ CINNAMON WHIPPED CREAM
Beat 1 cup heavy cream, ¼ cup confectioners' sugar and ½ teaspoon each **Ground Cinnamon** and **Pure Vanilla Extract** in medium bowl with electric mixer on medium speed until soft peaks form.

flavor variations

■ CHOCOLATE PECAN PIE
Prepare as directed. Melt 2 ounces semi-sweet chocolate as directed on package. Cool slightly. Stir into filling mixture before adding pecans.

■ VANILLA WALNUT PIE
Prepare as directed. Omit Ground Cinnamon. Use 1½ cups chopped walnuts in place of the pecan pieces.

Lemon Meringue Pie

PREP TIME: 25 minutes · **COOK TIME:** 20 minutes

1 cup sugar
¼ cup cornstarch
1½ cups cold water
3 egg yolks, slightly beaten
¼ cup lemon juice
1 tablespoon butter
½ teaspoon **Pure Lemon Extract**
1 baked pie crust (9-inch)

MERINGUE TOPPING:
⅓ cup sugar
½ teaspoon **Cream of Tartar**
3 egg whites
¼ teaspoon **Pure Lemon Extract**

MIX sugar and cornstarch in medium saucepan. Gradually stir in water until smooth. Stir in egg yolks. Stirring constantly, bring to boil on medium heat; boil 1 minute. Remove from heat. Stir in lemon juice, butter and Pure Lemon Extract. Pour hot filling into baked pie crust.

FOR the Meringue Topping, mix sugar and Cream of Tartar in small bowl. Beat egg whites in medium bowl with electric mixer on high speed until foamy. Gradually add sugar mixture and Pure Lemon Extract, beating until stiff peaks form. Spread meringue evenly over hot filling, sealing to edges of crust.

BAKE in preheated 350°F oven 15 to 20 minutes or until meringue is golden. Cool completely on wire rack.

► **MAKES 8 SERVINGS**

Easier Than Apple Pie

PREP TIME: 15 minutes · **COOK TIME:** 20 minutes

1 refrigerated pie crust (from 15-ounce
    package)
1 egg white, lightly beaten
¾ cup sugar
2 tablespoons cornstarch
2 teaspoons **Ground Cinnamon**
4 cups thinly sliced peeled apples (about
    4 medium)*
1 teaspoon sugar

* For best results, use Gala, Granny Smith <u>or</u>
Braeburn apples

PREPARE crust as directed on package. Place on foil-lined 12-inch pizza pan. If necessary, press out any folds or creases. Brush crust with about ½ of the beaten egg white.

MIX ¾ cup sugar, cornstarch and Ground Cinnamon in medium bowl. Toss with apples. Spoon into center of crust, spreading to within 2 inches of edges. Fold 2-inch edge of crust up over apples, pleating or folding crust as needed. Brush crust with remaining egg white; sprinkle with 1 teaspoon sugar.

BAKE in preheated 425°F oven 20 minutes or until apples are tender. Cool slightly before serving.

► **MAKES 8 SERVINGS**

flavor variations

■ SPICED EASIER THAN APPLE PIE
Prepare as directed. Use 1½ teaspoons **Pumpkin Pie Spice** <u>or</u> 1 teaspoon **Apple Pie Spice** in place of the Ground Cinnamon.

■ EASIER THAN PEAR PIE
Prepare as directed. Use 4 cups thinly sliced cored and peeled pears (about 4 pears) in place of the apples. Increase cornstarch to 3 tablespoons and add ½ teaspoon **Ground Ginger** with the Ground Cinnamon.

■ EASIER THAN APPLE & PEAR PIE
Prepare as directed. Use 2 cups <u>each</u> thinly sliced peeled and cored apples <u>and</u> pears and 1½ teaspoons **Ground Cinnamon** and ½ teaspoon **Ground Ginger** in place of the Ground Cinnamon.

■ Add ¼ cup raisins, dried cranberries <u>or</u> dried cherries to the fruit mixture.

Summer Fruit Tart

PREP TIME: 20 minutes · **COOK TIME:** 20 minutes

1 refrigerated pie crust (from 15-ounce package)
1 egg white, lightly beaten
⅓ cup sugar
2 tablespoons cornstarch
½ teaspoon **Ground Cinnamon**
¼ teaspoon **Ground Ginger**
2 cups peeled, seeded and sliced peaches
1 cup blueberries
½ teaspoon **Pure Vanilla Extract**

PREPARE crust as directed on package. Place on foil-lined 12-inch pizza pan. Spray with nonstick cooking spray. If necessary, press out any folds or creases. Brush crust with about ½ of the beaten egg white.

MIX sugar, cornstarch, Ground Cinnamon and Ground Ginger in large bowl. Add fruit and Pure Vanilla Extract; toss gently. Spoon into center of crust, spreading to within 2 inches of edges. Fold 2-inch edge of crust up over fruit, pleating or folding crust as needed. Brush crust with remaining egg white.

BAKE in preheated 425°F oven 20 minutes or until crust is golden brown. Cool slightly before serving.

► **MAKES 8 SERVINGS**

Pear and Cranberry Crumble Pie

PREP TIME: 20 minutes · **COOK TIME:** 1 hour

1 refrigerated pie crust (from 15-ounce
package)
¾ cup granulated sugar
3 tablespoons cornstarch
1 teaspoon **Ground Cinnamon,** divided
¼ teaspoon **Ground Allspice,** divided
6 firm ripe pears, cored, peeled and sliced
¾ cups dried cranberries
½ cup flour
¼ cup firmly packed light brown sugar
¼ cup (½ stick) cold butter, cut into chunks

PREPARE pie crust as directed on package for 1-crust pie using 9-inch pie plate.

MIX granulated sugar, cornstarch, ½ teaspoon of the Ground Cinnamon and ⅛ teaspoon of the Ground Allspice in large bowl. Add pears and cranberries; toss to coat well. Spoon evenly into crust.

MIX flour, brown sugar, remaining ½ teaspoon Ground Cinnamon and ⅛ teaspoon Ground Allspice in small bowl. Cut in butter with pastry blender or 2 knives until coarse crumbs form. Sprinkle evenly over fruit in crust. Place pie on large baking sheet.

BAKE in preheated 375°F oven 1 hour or until pears are tender and topping is lightly browned. Cool on wire rack.

► **MAKES 10 SERVINGS**

flavor variations

■ **APPLE AND CRANBERRY
CRUMBLE PIE**
Prepare as directed. Use 6 apples, peeled, cored and sliced, in place of the pears.

■ **GINGER PEAR AND CRANBERRY
CRUMBLE PIE**
Prepare as directed. Omit Ground Cinnamon and Ground Allspice. Use ½ teaspoon **Ground Ginger** in the pear mixture and ½ teaspoon **Ground Ginger** in the crumb topping.

Ground Allspice

Holiday

Family and friends will **savor** these **delicious** twists on

holiday **classics**.

Savory Herb-Rub Roasted Turkey

PREP TIME: 20 minutes · **COOK TIME:** 3½ hours

2 tablespoons **Poultry Seasoning**
1 tablespoon **Season-All® Seasoned Salt**
1 tablespoon **Paprika**
2 teaspoons **Garlic Powder**
1 teaspoon **Ground Black Pepper**
¾ teaspoon **Ground Nutmeg**
1 whole turkey (12 to 14 pounds), fresh or
   frozen, thawed
1 large onion, cut into wedges
6 **Bay Leaves**
1 tablespoon vegetable oil
½ cup water

PLACE oven rack in lowest position. Place roasting rack in shallow roasting pan. Mix Poultry Seasoning, Season-All Seasoned Salt, Paprika, Garlic Powder, Ground Black Pepper and Ground Nutmeg in small bowl.

RINSE turkey; pat dry. Place turkey, breast side up, in prepared pan. Sprinkle half of the seasoning mixture inside turkey. Stuff with onion and Bay Leaves. Brush turkey breast with oil. Spread remaining seasoning mixture over entire surface and under skin of turkey. Add water to pan; cover loosely with heavy-duty foil.

ROAST in preheated 325°F oven 1 hour. Remove foil. Basting occasionally with pan juices, roast 2 to 2½ hours longer or until internal temperature of the breast reaches 165°F (175°F in thigh). Remove turkey from oven. Let stand 20 minutes. Transfer to platter or carving board to slice. Reserve pan juices to make Perfect Turkey Gravy, if desired (see recipe below), or to serve with turkey.

► **MAKES 12 SERVINGS**

flavor additions

■ PERFECT TURKEY GRAVY
Mix 2 packages **Turkey Gravy Mix** and ¼ cup flour in large saucepan. Gradually stir in 3 cups cold water and 1 cup turkey drippings <u>or</u> turkey broth with whisk until smooth. Stirring frequently, cook on medium-high heat until gravy comes to boil. Reduce heat to low and simmer 5 minutes or until thickened, stirring occasionally. (Gravy will continue to thicken upon standing.)

■ PERFECT TURKEY GRAVY WITH SAGE
Stir ½ teaspoon **Rubbed Sage** into Gravy Mix.

■ PERFECT TURKEY GRAVY WITH POULTRY SEASONING
Stir ¼ teaspoon Poultry Seasoning into Gravy Mix.

Spinach Salad with Lemon & Pepper Dressing

PREP TIME: 15 minutes

½ cup olive oil
2 tablespoons vinegar
1 tablespoon sugar
2 teaspoons **Lemon & Pepper Seasoning Salt**
2 packages (5 to 6 ounces <u>each</u>) spinach leaves
1 cup sliced mushrooms
Crumbled cooked bacon, chopped hard-cooked eggs, sliced red onion and croutons

MIX oil, vinegar, sugar and Lemon & Pepper Seasoning Salt in small bowl with wire whisk until well blended.

TOSS spinach and mushrooms in large bowl. Top with bacon, egg, onion and croutons. Serve with Lemon & Pepper Dressing.

► **MAKES 10 SERVINGS**

flavor variations

■ HONEY VINAIGRETTE
Mix ½ cup olive oil, ¼ cup white wine vinegar, 2 tablespoons honey, ½ teaspoon **Garlic Powder**, ¼ teaspoon **Ground Black Pepper** and 1 teaspoon **Poppy Seed** (optional) in small bowl with wire whisk until well blended.

flavor additions

■ Sliced strawberries, orange segments, sliced avocado and toasted pecans or walnuts make wonderful additions to Spinach Salad.

Classic Herb Stuffing

PREP TIME: 15 minutes · **COOK TIME:** 40 minutes

1 cup (2 sticks) butter
2 cups chopped celery
1 cup chopped onion
2 teaspoons **Thyme Leaves**
1½ teaspoons **Poultry Seasoning**
1 teaspoon **Season-All® Seasoned Salt**
½ teaspoon **Ground Black Pepper**
12 cups dry unseasoned bread cubes
4 cups chicken broth

MELT butter in large skillet on medium heat. Add celery and onion; cook and stir 5 minutes. Stir in Thyme Leaves, Poultry Seasoning, Season-All Seasoned Salt and Ground Black Pepper.

PLACE bread cubes in large bowl. Add celery mixture and broth; toss gently until well mixed. Spoon into lightly greased 13x9-inch baking dish.

BAKE in preheated 375°F oven 35 minutes or until heated through and lightly browned.

► **MAKES 18 SERVINGS**

Thyme Leaves

Poultry Seasoning

Spicy Nutmeg Carrots

PREP TIME: 5 minutes · **COOK TIME:** 5 minutes

1 package (16 ounces) baby carrots
2 tablespoons butter, melted
¼ teaspoon **Ground Nutmeg**
¼ teaspoon **Garlic Salt**
⅛ teaspoon **Ground Red Pepper**

COOK carrots as directed on package.

MIX butter, Ground Nutmeg, Garlic Salt and Ground Red Pepper in small bowl. Pour over carrots; toss to coat well. Serve immediately.

► **MAKES 5 SERVINGS**

Roasted Sweet Potatoes with Cinnamon Pecan Crunch

PREP TIME: 15 minutes · **COOK TIME:** 1 hour

½ cup firmly packed brown sugar, divided
2 tablespoons orange juice
2 teaspoons **Pure Vanilla Extract**
1½ teaspoons **Ground Cinnamon,** divided
½ teaspoon salt
3 pounds sweet potatoes, peeled and cut
   into 1-inch chunks
1 cup dried cranberries
4 tablespoons butter, divided
¼ cup flour
1 cup chopped pecans

MIX ¼ cup of the brown sugar, orange juice, Pure Vanilla Extract, 1 teaspoon of the Ground Cinnamon and salt in large bowl. Add sweet potatoes and cranberries; toss to coat well. Spoon into 13x9-inch baking dish. Dot with 2 tablespoons of the butter. Cover with foil. Bake in preheated 400°F oven 30 minutes.

MEANWHILE, mix flour, remaining ¼ cup brown sugar and remaining ½ teaspoon Ground Cinnamon in medium bowl. Cut in remaining 2 tablespoons butter with a fork until coarse crumbs form. Stir in pecans. Remove sweet potatoes from oven and stir gently. Sprinkle with pecan topping.

BAKE, uncovered, 25 to 30 minutes longer or until sweet potatoes are tender and topping is lightly browned.

► **MAKES 8 SERVINGS**

Ground Cinnamon

Sage and Cheddar Potato Gratin

PREP TIME: 30 minutes · **COOK TIME:** 1 hour

2 teaspoons **Rubbed Sage**
1½ teaspoons salt
½ teaspoon **Ground Black Pepper**
3 pounds potatoes, peeled and thinly sliced
1 large onion, thinly sliced
2 cups shredded Cheddar cheese
1 cup chicken broth
1 cup heavy cream

MIX Rubbed Sage, salt and Ground Black Pepper in small bowl. Layer ⅓ of the potatoes and ½ of the onion in lightly greased 13x9-inch baking dish. Sprinkle with 1 teaspoon of the sage mixture and ⅓ of the cheese. Repeat layers. Top with remaining potatoes, sage mixture and cheese.

STIR broth and cream in medium bowl with wire whisk until well blended. Pour evenly over potatoes.

BAKE in preheated 400°F oven 1 hour or until potatoes are tender and top is golden. Let stand 5 minutes before serving.

► **MAKES 12 SERVINGS**

Black Peppercorns

Sage

Red Velvet Cake with Vanilla Cream Cheese Frosting

PREP TIME: 20 minutes · **COOK TIME:** 40 minutes

2½ cups flour
½ cup cocoa powder
1 teaspoon baking soda
½ teaspoon salt
1 cup (2 sticks) butter, softened
2 cups granulated sugar
4 eggs
1 cup (8 ounces) sour cream
½ cup milk
1 bottle (1 ounce) **Red Food Color**
2 teaspoons **Pure Vanilla Extract**

VANILLA CREAM CHEESE FROSTING:
1 package (8 ounces) cream cheese,
  softened
¼ cup (½ stick) butter, softened
2 tablespoons sour cream
2 teaspoons **Pure Vanilla Extract**
1 package (16 ounces) confectioners' sugar

SIFT flour, cocoa powder, baking soda and salt; set aside. Beat butter and sugar in large bowl with electric mixer on high speed 5 to 7 minutes or until light and fluffy. Beat in eggs, one at a time. Mix in sour cream, milk, Red Food Color and Pure Vanilla Extract. Gradually beat in flour mixture on low speed just until blended. Do not overbeat.

POUR batter into 2 greased and floured 9-inch round cake pans.

BAKE in preheated 350° F oven 35 to 40 minutes or until toothpick inserted in center comes out clean. Cool 10 minutes; remove from pans. Cool completely on wire rack.

FOR THE FROSTING, beat cream cheese, butter and sour cream in large bowl until smooth. Mix in Pure Vanilla Extract. Gradually beat in confectioners' sugar on medium speed until light and fluffy. Fill and frost cake layers with frosting.

► **MAKES 16 SERVINGS**

The Enspicelopedia™

Everything you've ever wanted to know about the **herbs** and **spices** you love.

Almond Extract

DESCRIPTION
Almond Extract is a flavoring produced by combining bitter-almond oil with ethyl alcohol. The almonds are heated, then the oils are extracted and combined with alcohol.

USES
Pure almond flavoring is a baker's must. Because it is clear, it will not add any color and can be used to lend a delightfully nutty flavor to confections and baked goods.

FLAVOR & AROMA PROFILE
Almond Extract has a strong nutty fragrance and a sweet almond flavor. The flavor is very intense, so it should be used sparingly.

ORIGINS & FOLKLORE
Almonds were among the earliest cultivated foods; there is evidence that they were grown before 3,000 B.C.

When Arab traders settled in Portugal and Spain, they imported citrus and almond trees from their homelands. Eventually, almonds became a common part of the cuisine in Spain and Portugal.

In the 1700s, Franciscan monks brought almond trees from Spain to California, and today, the San Joaquin and Sacramento Valleys are the chief almond-growing centers in the United States.

In classical times Romans presented gifts of sugared almonds to important dignitaries as well as personal friends. At weddings guests tossed almonds at the bride and groom as a symbol of fertility.

Basil

DESCRIPTION
Basil is a member of the mint family. Its botanical name is derived from the Greek "to be fragrant."

FLAVOR & AROMA PROFILE
Basil has a fresh, clean fragrance with green, minty flavor notes.

USES
Basil is used in many Mediterranean dishes. It is used in green Thai curry blend, bouquet garni and Italian seasonings.

ORIGINS & FOLKLORE
Basil is believed to have originated in India, where it still grows wild.

In ancient Egypt, Basil was used in the embalming and mummification process. Through the centuries, it became a custom of young Italian suitors to wear a sprig of

The Difference Between Spices and Herbs

Often, the word *spice* is used as a general name for all dried flavorings. But did you know that herbs and spices are two very different things?

Spices are the dried bark, seeds or roots of plants. They are usually sold ground, but many of them can be found in their whole forms as well.

Herbs are the leafy green parts of a plant; they are available both fresh and dried. When they are sold dried, they are usually chopped (like basil) or rubbed (such as sage).

Dried herbs tend to have more intense flavor than fresh; the quality is also more consistent year-round, while fresh herbs tend to fluctuate in flavor and quality throughout the year.

Basil as a sign of their marital intentions. In India, Hindus believed that if a leaf of Basil were buried with them, it would serve as their passport to heaven.

Bay Leaves

DESCRIPTION
Bay Leaves are the dried leaves of an evergreen tree.

FLAVOR & AROMA PROFILE
Bay Leaves' aromatic flavor is pungent and spicy, with cooling undertones and a pleasantly mild bitter aftertaste.

USES
Bay Leaves are an essential ingredient in winter's warming meals, such as soups and stews. They are also used in Mediterranean, Indian, Middle Eastern and Caribbean cuisines.

ORIGINS & FOLKLORE
Bay Leaves are native to the Mediterranean area. Bay Leaves grown in Turkey are considered the finest in the world.

Champions of the Olympic games in ancient Greece wore garlands of Bay Leaves. Our word *baccalaureate* alludes to the bay wreaths worn by poets and scholars

when they received academic honors in ancient Greece.

Black Pepper

DESCRIPTION
Black Peppercorns are the dried berries of a vine. The berries are picked while still green, allowed to ferment and are then sun-dried until they shrivel and turn a brownish-black color.

FLAVOR & AROMA PROFILE
Black Pepper has a sharp, penetrating aroma and a characteristic woody, piney flavor.

USES

Black Pepper adds flavor to almost every food of every nation in the world. It is used in rubs, spice blends, salad dressings and peppercorn blends.

FOLKLORE

Black Pepper is considered the "king of the spices" by many spice buyers due to its popularity and historical significance. Pepper was so precious in ancient times that it was used as money to pay taxes, tributes, dowries and rent. In 410 A.D., when Rome was captured, 3,000 pounds of pepper were demanded as ransom.

Chili Powder

DESCRIPTION

Chili Powder is a combination of ground chiles, cumin, oregano, garlic and salt.

FLAVOR & AROMA PROFILE

Chili Powder lends smoky and spicy flavor to all kinds of dishes.

USES

Chili Powder is the essential flavoring ingredient in chili. It can also be used to add Southwestern flavor to bean dishes, guacamole and baked goods.

Cinnamon

DESCRIPTION

Cinnamon is the dried inner bark of various species of evergreen trees. At harvest, the bark is stripped off and put in the sun, where it curls into the quill shape that we know as cinnamon sticks.

FLAVOR & AROMA PROFILE

Cinnamon is characteristically woody, musty and earthy in flavor and aroma.

USES

Cinnamon is popular in sweet baked dishes, with fruits and in confections. Cinnamon is also widely used in savory dishes around the world such as moles, curries, tagines and barbecue.

ORIGINS & FOLKLORE

Cinnamon imported from Indonesia is the most common form sold in the United States. It has a milder red-hot flavor followed by a pleasantly woody note. Vietnam is the source for Saigon Cinnamon, which is considered the finest variety available and has a bold spicy-sweet flavor.

The word cinnamon means "sweet wood" in Malay. The Romans believed Cinnamon to be sacred and burned it at funerals.

Cinnamon was one of the first spices sought in the 15th Century European explorations, and some say it indirectly led to the discovery of America.

Cumin

DESCRIPTION
Cumin is the dried seed of an herb that is a member of the parsley family.

FLAVOR & AROMA PROFILE
Cumin has by a pungent earthy flavor.

USES
The flavor of Cumin plays a major role in Mexican, Thai, Vietnamese and Indian cuisines. Cumin is a critical ingredient of chili powder, and is found in adobos, garam masala and curry powder.

FOLKLORE
Superstition during the Middle Ages cited that Cumin kept chickens and lovers from wandering. It was also believed that a happy life awaited the bride and groom who carried Cumin Seed throughout the wedding.

Dill

DESCRIPTION
Dill is a member of the parsley family and is related to Anise, Caraway, Coriander, Cumin and Fennel. Dill Weed is the dried leaves of the same plant from which Dill Seed comes.

FLAVOR & AROMA PROFILE
Dill Weed has a more subtle, fresh flavor than the seeds. It is characterized by sweet, tea-like and rye notes; the seeds tend to be warmer in flavor.

USES
European and American cuisines use Dill Seed in pickles, meats, seafood, cheeses and breads. Dill Weed is also used with fish and shellfish.

FOLKLORE
Dill's name comes from the Old Norse *dilla,* meaning "to lull," and was once given to crying babies. Dill is also thought to cure hiccups, stomachaches, insomnia and bad breath. The most famous use of Dill, the Dill pickle, is at least 400 years old.

Ginger

DESCRIPTION
Ginger is the underground stem of a plant that grows 2 to 3 feet tall.

FLAVOR & AROMA PROFILE
The flavor of Ginger is a unique combination of citrus, soapy and earthy flavor notes.

USES
Ginger is used in baked goods, curries and in spice blends around the world.

FOLKLORE
Ginger's name is derived from a Sanskrit word meaning "horn-shaped" or "horn-root." During the 15th century, gingerbread became a gift of love and respect. In the 1800's, Ginger was commonly sprinkled on top of beer or ale, then stirred into the drink with a hot poker—thus the invention of ginger ale.

Intensify the Flavor of Seed Spices
Chefs have long prized seeds for their fresh flavor and aroma, which are released at the moment the seed is ground or crushed. An easy way to intensify the flavor of seed spices is to toast them before using them in a recipe.

1. Heat a dry skillet over medium heat.
2. Once skillet is hot, pour in desired amount of seeds.
3. Using a spatula, stir the seeds in the pan until they become fragrant, approximately 1 to 2 minutes.

Lemon Extract

DESCRIPTION
Lemon Extract is made by pressing the outer peel, which contains the lemon oil, and combining the oil with ethyl alcohol.

USES
Mostly used in baking (especially cheesecakes and often mixed with lemon zest), or added to fish and poultry marinades. Also used in glazes, frostings and candy-making.

FLAVOR & AROMA PROFILE
Lemon Extract has a strong, clear lemon aroma and true lemon flavor.

FOLKLORE
Lemons were once used by the British Royal navy to combat scurvy, a disease caused by a deficiency of vitamin C.

Nutmeg

DESCRIPTION
Nutmeg is the seed of the same fruit from which Mace is derived.

Vanilla
Vanilla is derived from the dried, cured beans or fruit pods of a member of the orchid family, this is the only orchid that produces edible fruit. Although Vanilla beans are sometimes used in their whole form, they are most commonly used for producing extracts and flavors.

Vanilla has a delicate, sweet and rich flavor and a spicy, recognizable fragrance.

Vanilla is used as a flavoring principally in sweet foods, and also as a fragrantly tenacious ingredient in perfumery.

Vanilla was enjoyed by the Aztecs in a drink called *xoco-lall*, which was made from cocoa and Vanilla beans. The explorer Cortéz sampled this drink and returned to Spain with reports that it contained magical powers.

FLAVOR & AROMA PROFILE
Nutmeg's oval-shaped seeds have a sweet, spicy flavor.

USES
Nutmeg enhances both sweet and savory foods. Nutmeg blends well with other

spices and is found in cuisines of countries around the globe including Italy, the Caribbean, France, India, Germany, Scandinavia, Greece, Latin America and the Middle East.

FOLKLORE
In colonial times, peddlers sold whittled wooden "nutmegs" to unsuspecting housewives.

Paprika

DESCRIPTION
Paprika is the dried, ground pods of a sweet red pepper. It is prized for its brilliant color.

FLAVOR & AROMA PROFILE
Most Paprika is mild and slightly sweet in flavor with a pleasantly fragrant aroma. Unlike regular Spanish Paprika which is well known for the visual appearance it gives to dishes, Smoked Paprika is known for its smoky-sweet flavor profile. Derived from naturally smoked sweet red peppers, this Smoked Paprika provides a fantastic smoked flavor and brilliant red color to items such as chicken, beef, potatoes and rice.

USES
Paprika is used in seasoning blends and the cuisines of India, Morocco, Europe and the Middle East.

FOLKLORE
Spanish explorers took red pepper seeds back to Europe, where the plant evolved into "sweet" Paprika. Pound for pound, Paprika has more vitamin-C than citrus fruit.

Rosemary

DESCRIPTION
The slender, slightly curved leaves of Rosemary resemble miniature curved pine needles. Rosemary grows under harsh mountainous conditions.

FLAVOR & AROMA PROFILE
Rosemary has a distinctive pine-woody aroma with a fresh, bittersweet flavor.

USES
Rosemary is found in bouquet garni, herbes de Provence and seasoning blends for lamb and Mediterranean cuisines.

FOLKLORE
In ancient Greece, Rosemary was valued for its alleged ability to strengthen the brain and memory. Also known as the "herb of remembrance," it was placed on the graves of English heroes.

Saffron

DESCRIPTION
Saffron is the dried yellow stigmas of a flower in the Iris family. It takes 225,000 of them to make 1 pound of saffron.

FLAVOR & AROMA PROFILE
Saffron is used sparingly because its odor and flavor are so strong. The taste is spicy, pleasantly bitter and slightly honey-like.

USES
Saffron is used in spice blends for paella, curry, kheer and bouillabaisse.

ORIGINS & FOLKLORE
Spain is considered the premium source of Saffron.

Saffron is the most expensive spice in the world. The ancient Assyrians used saffron for medicinal purposes. The Greeks and Romans used it to perfume their luxurious baths. The bright orange-yellow color also made saffron useful as a dye.

Sage

DESCRIPTION
Sage's leaves are silvery green in color.

Cut Sage refers to leaves that have been cut rather than ground into smaller pieces. Rubbed Sage is put through minimum grinding and a coarse sieve. The result is a fluffy, almost cotton-like product, unique among ground herbs. More Sage is sold in the rubbed form than any other.

FLAVOR & AROMA PROFILE

Sage is highly aromatic and is characterized by a medicinal, piney-woody flavor.

USES

Sage is used in Greek, Italian and European cuisines. It is used to season sausages, poultry and fish.

ORIGINS & FOLKLORE

Historically, Southeastern Europe has been the principal producer of Sage. Dalmatian Sage, as it is commonly called, has been recognized as superior in the United States. It is highly aromatic, noted for its mellowness. Its smoother taste is due to differing essential oil components.

Sage has been traditionally used for its antioxidant and antimicrobial properties. Sage was used during the Middle Ages to treat maladies such as fevers, liver disease and epilepsy. One common belief was that Sage strengthened the memory, hence a sage, or wise man, always had a long memory. During the 1600s, the Chinese exchanged three to four pounds of their tea with Dutch traders for one pound of European sage leaves.

OLD BAY® Seasoning

OLD BAY Seasoning is a mixture of more than a dozen herbs and spices, including celery, bay leaves, mustard, red pepper and ginger. OLD BAY's flavor is pungent, earthy and citrusy, and warming to taste.

OLD BAY Seasoning was created in 1939 by Gustav Brunn, a German immigrant with dreams of starting a spice business. Originally available only in the Chesapeake Bay area, OLD BAY's popularity has spread across the United States and Canada.

Once the preferred seasoning for crabs and shrimp, OLD BAY is now popular in non-seafood dishes as well. Hamburgers, fried chicken and gumbo are now also flavored with OLD BAY.

Montreal Steak® Seasoning

A bold blend of black pepper, garlic and select spices, Montreal Steak Seasoning is known as "the flavor you can see." This chunky blend will make you the master of the grill, and give you that special ingredient all your friends and family will ask for.

Index

173

Conversion Table for Cooking

VOLUME

1 teaspoon = 5 mL
1 tablespoon = 15 mL
1 fluid ounce = 30 mL
1 cup = 240 mL
2 cups (1 pint) = 470 mL
4 cups (1 quart) = 0.95 liter
4 quarts (1 gallon) = 3.8 liters

WEIGHT

1 ounce = 28 grams
1 pound = 454 grams

AREA

¼ inch = 6 mm
½ inch = 1 cm
1 inch = 3 cm

TEMPERATURE

°F	°C
225	110
250	120
275	135
300	150
325	160
350	180
375	190
400	205
425	220
450	230
475	245
500	260